James Dickey and
the Politics of Canon

Ernest Suarez

James Dickey and the Politics of Canon

Assessing the Savage Ideal

University of Missouri Press
Columbia and London

5   4   3   2   1   97   96   95   94   93

Library of Congress Cataloging-in-Publication Data

Suarez, Ernest.

   James Dickey and the politics of canon : assessing the savage
 ideal / Ernest Suarez.

      p.   cm.

   Includes bibliographical references and index.

   ISBN 0-8262-0921-1 (alk. paper)

      1. Dickey, James—Criticism and interpretation—History.

   2. Politics and literature—United States—History—20th century.

   3. Canon (Literature)   I. Title.

   PS3554.I32Z87   1993   93-29880

   811'.54—dc20   CIP

∞™ This paper meets the requirements of the
American National Standard for Permanence of Paper
for Printed Library Materials, Z39.48, 1984.

Designer: Kristie Lee
Typesetter: Connell-Zeko Type & Graphics
Printer and Binder: Thomson-Shore, Inc.
Typefaces: Palatino and Bauhaus

For my lovely Anna, and our dudes, Ernest
and Christopher, who know how to rock 'n' roll
For Tom, who got "The Hit"

Contents

Acknowledgments

This book was a pleasure to write, largely because of the people who helped along the way. First and foremost, I would like to tip my glass to Thomas Hill Schaub, a most brilliant critic of contemporary literature and, more importantly, a loving and loyal friend. Tom provided necessary and invaluable conceptual and practical assistance at every stage of the manuscript's development. Whether we were sitting drinking beer in the Memorial Union at the University of Wisconsin or talking long-distance—Madison to D.C.—he always did everything within his power to help. What can I say? Tom, you're a star.

I also owe a great debt to the other people on whom I have always counted for personal and professional help and advice. Sargent Bush, Jr., read most of the manuscript and provided very valuable criticism. Despite his perverted fanaticism for the Boston Red Sox, he has always been an inspiration to me, and I love him like a father. Lawrence Broer has long been a role model and a soul mate. His insightful and appreciative reading of the manuscript in its final stages was the basis for some important fine-tuning. Virgil Nemoainu read parts of the manuscript and made perceptive suggestions. Our regular conversations always greatly benefited me. Lynn Keller read the manuscript at an early stage and helped me get beyond the rough spots. I spent countless hours with Phil Gould, Jonathan Little, Michael "de Bum" Van den Heuvel, and Christopher Wheatley talking about Dickey's work, their own books, and other things literary, while we cranked up the Allman Brothers, the Maker's Mark, and the Wild Goose. A special thanks goes to James Dickey for providing me with interviews and access to his unpublished papers.

Beverly Jarrett, the Director and Editor-in-Chief of the University of Missouri Press, has been nothing short of wonderful. George Adams, William Andrews, Dale Bauer, Harriet and Irving Deer, Richard Dietrich, Rosemary Gates, Phillip Herring, Mark Hodin, Gordon Hutner, Herb Karl, D. B. Kelly, Robert Kirschten, John O. Lyons, Joyce Pair, Walter Rideout, Lawrence Rodgers, Joseph Sendry, and Brother Rick Wilson provided friendship and various kinds of advice. Tim Fox did a splendid job of editing the manuscript. Jane Lago and Bridget Lacey helped prepare the manuscript. Helen Sugarman took the author's photo. The Catholic University of America and the University of Wisconsin at Madison and at Whitewater furnished me with facilities, fellowships, and grants. I would like to thank the library staffs at these institutions, as well as at the University of South Carolina and the Library of Congress, for assistance.

Finally, I would like to thank those whom I love the most, my family. My mother and father lost everything, came to this country penniless, and dug their way out of the New York City slums in order to build successful lives and educate their children. My wife's father busted his back at two jobs a day to do the same for her. My brother, Carlos, and my ninety-three-year-old *abuela* are always there when I need them. My wife, Anna, and our kids, Ernest and Christopher, are the best partners with whom anyone could ever go through life.

Salud to you all!

Abbreviations

The following abbreviations appear parenthetically throughout the text and notes to identify frequently cited works by James Dickey.

"BP"   "Barnstorming for Poetry"
CM   *The Central Motion*
"EM"   "The Energized Man"
"IG"   "The Imagination as Glory"
IS   *Into the Stone and Other Poems*
MA   *Metaphor as Pure Adventure: A Lecture Delivered at the Library of Congress, December 4, 1967*
NH   *Night Hurdling*
SI   *Self-Interviews*
S   *Sorties*
SC   *Spinning the Crystal Ball*
SP   *The Suspect in Poetry*
VC   *The Voiced Connections of James Dickey*

James Dickey and
the Politics of Canon

Introduction

This book is a historical examination of the relationship of the James Dickey oeuvre to contemporary literary, ideological, and cultural pressures. The dramatic rise of Dickey's literary reputation in the sixties and his equally abrupt fall from critical grace after the early seventies is the most distinctive feature of his career. How is it possible, within less than ten years, for a writer to go from being hailed as the most important poet of his time to being virtually ignored in assessments of post–World War II poetic history? I seek to answer that question by investigating the development of Dickey's writing, public image, and critical reputation within the context of contemporary poetry and the ideological underpinnings of assessments of post–World War II American poetic history. Critical assessments of Dickey's place in literary history strongly suggest the politics underlying the changes that have taken— and continue to take—place in literary criticism. I use Dickey's career to explore how a critical reputation is built and dismantled, and to investigate the historical origins for the changes in recent critics' criteria for deciding an author's importance.

The organization of chapters 1 through 4 is largely chronological: each chapter concerns a dominant aesthetic mode characteristic of Dickey's career at a specific stage. Further, my examination of Dickey's aesthetic assumes his writing and critical reputation cannot be understood without taking into account his creation of a public image

and his use of the multiple poetic selves, or personae, that inhabit
his poems. Since a primary objective of this study is to locate Dickey
within a broad historical perspective, each chapter frames Dickey's
aesthetic and thematic concerns in a different cultural and literary
context. Chapter 1 considers Dickey's experimentations with mod-
ernist techniques in the fifties. Through an examination of Dickey's
early uncollected poems and of his correspondence with Ezra Pound,
I look at Dickey's relationship with modernism and New Criticism.
In Chapter 2 I demonstrate how the escalation of the Vietnam War
affected the directions visionary poetry took in the sixties. I discuss
critical reactions to Dickey's use of violence and detail his relation-
ship with Robert Bly in order to place Dickey's and others' poetry
(especially work associated with the deep image school) in the con-
text of American visionary poetry. Chapter 3 analyzes how recent
critics' opinions of Dickey's work reveal the ways in which the
Vietnam and post-Vietnam milieu have influenced the various di-
rections literary criticism has taken, and how changes in critics'
criteria have affected appraisals of Dickey's place in the contem-
porary literary canon. Chapter 4 demonstrates how recent critics
have identified confessionalism, and other movements that advocate
doing away with persona, as the dominant contemporary poetic
modes, causing critics often to associate Dickey with the various
personae he adapts. Looking at Dickey's use of personae and the
critical responses to his work shows how critics' assumptions have
led to widespread misinterpretations of Dickey's examination of the
"savage ideal"—the relationship between romanticism and hedo-
nism—in his poetry and fiction.

Before examining these developments in Dickey's writing and
the critical reactions to them, I will discuss a number of more gen-
eral factors concerning Dickey's relationship to the post–World
War II literary milieu. Such an overview will allow me to avoid
occasionally digressing in order to provide relevant background
information for those not familiar with contemporary poetry or
with the public image Dickey has cultivated.

Classifying Dickey is not easy because he fits into none of the
post–World War II poetic movements, such as beat, confessional,
Black Mountain, deep image, or New York school, and because he

has encouraged critics to view him as an independent figure. Dickey has carefully used a variety of formats to project a public image that distinguishes him not only from his modernist ancestors—a quality shared by many post–World War II poets—but also from his contemporaries. Because Dickey has always been willing—even eager—to comment on his own work and goals, the shape of his career, other writers' work, and the state of contemporary letters, the critic has available Dickey's opinion on practically anything Dickey ever wrote or, for that matter, practically anything that has occurred in contemporary letters since World War II. Indeed, in his criticism, journals, and prefaces, Dickey often attempts to do the work of the critic by defining the major phases or, as he calls them, the major "Motions" of his development.

This characteristic is hardly unique to Dickey, of course. Writers as different as Whitman, Clemens, Stein, Hemingway, Rich, Ginsberg, Bly, and Mailer have all engaged in active self-advertising in order to secure their places in literary history. Like many of these other writers, Dickey uses "nonfiction" formats to invite biographical interpretations of his prose fiction and of his poetry, as when he writes in a journal entry in *Sorties* (1971), "I am Lewis," referring to a character in *Deliverance* (75). In such cases it becomes difficult in the final assessment to view Dickey's work outside of the context of the image he projects. But critics are too often disposed to either completely accept or completely reject Dickey's statements, rather than examining the interaction between the image Dickey cultivates and his writing.[1]

Moreover, because of the consistency of Dickey's subject matter, the vast majority of critics over the years have limited themselves to thematic explications of his poetry, and little or none of this critical attention has attempted to put Dickey in a cultural context. Critics' failure to place Dickey in a cultural context is especially noteworthy because his work reflects a wide spectrum of currents that run through recent American culture. As Joyce Carol Oates points out, "Even more than Whitman, Dickey contains multitudes."[2] Further-

---

1. Neal Bowers's study *James Dickey: The Poet as Pitchman* looks at Dickey's role as a salesman or "pitchman" for poetry, but it does not examine the complexity of the relationship between Dickey's public image and his poetry and fiction.

2. "Out of the Stone, into the Flesh: The Imagination of James Dickey," 206.

more, like Whitman, Dickey does not offer moral judgments, a fact
sometimes resulting in charges of a lack of social consciousness, but
searches to understand and commune with the "multitudes" he
embraces. Through his use of this perspective we discover in the
Dickey oeuvre the violence, sexism, racism, compassion, egotism,
despair, hope, and guilt that continue to storm in contemporary
America's collective consciousness.

Dickey's use of the perspective of the "common" American man
is one of the most important factors that distinguishes his work
from that of Charles Olson, Ginsberg, Rich, Lowell, and others,
which was written as they were striving to break away from mod-
ernist poetics. Like Dickey, these poets wrote poetry that was di-
rectly "in-touch-with" life; nevertheless, they differed significantly
from Dickey because the form and subject matter of their verse
were less representative of the cultural mainstream. Olson's *Max-
imus Poems* were idiosyncratic, obscure, and often seemingly for-
mally anarchic. Ginsberg catered to a counterculture that blatantly
rejected mainstream values. Rich advocated radically feminist posi-
tions. Lowell was far less socially radical in his verse than Olson,
Ginsberg, or Rich—though he shared their antiwar sentiments—
but was markedly upper-class, genetically tied to one of America's
most well known families.

Lowell's considerable literary talent aside, one of the reasons he
was early identified as *the* poet who broke away from modernist
poetics is that he wrote verse from a perspective culturally recog-
nizable to a wide academic audience; yet however culturally recog-
nizable the sensibility behind *Life Studies* is, it does not present—or
pretend to present—a world that could be called "middle Ameri-
can." One section of the book contains poems full of references to—
and in some cases personal reminiscences of—Ford Madox Ford,
George Santayana, Delmore Schwartz, and Hart Crane, while the
famous final section presents a world peopled by Lowell's well-
known relatives and makes references to Harvard and the Sunday
Yacht Club. Though the less self-consciously crafted, more subjec-
tive and conversational form of *Life Studies* does indicate a move
away from T. S. Eliot and Allen Tate, the subject matter of the verse
retains its intellectual, elitist appeal.

Dickey, on the other hand, desired to write poetry with integrity that could speak to people by appealing to the cultural mainstream. While his work does sometimes show dissatisfaction with the world he explores, he examines mainstream America not from a counter-cultural or an "outsider's" perspective but from the "inside" (a point to which I will return in detail in subsequent chapters). Accordingly, Dickey has created a public personality to match this perspective by projecting an image distinctly different from that of other poets. Looking at the literary milieu he discovered when he returned from combat duty in the Pacific in 1946 helps situate where that image fits into the history of contemporary American poetry.

The literary climate from which Dickey emerged was dominated by Eliot, Pound, and William Carlos Williams, who had all become, in James Breslin's words, "canonized revolutionaries."[3] Indeed, poets as different as Lowell, Olson, and Ginsberg have expressed dismay and anxiety about the possibility of breaking away from the omnipresent shadows of the major moderns. Lowell wondered whether he and his contemporaries were fated to be the "uncomfortable epigoni of Frost, Pound, Eliot, Marianne Moore, etc." Olson expressed anxiety about being able "to keep my own ego above their [the major modernists'] water." Ginsberg described—in an entry from his notebook during the time he was writing "Howl," a poem that represented a break from modernist poetics—a dream in which Eliot asks him to read, and Ginsberg weeps in gratitude for Eliot's recognition.[4]

Ginsberg's dream typifies the dilemma that confronted many of the new generation of poets who emerged after World War II: while on the one hand they desperately strove to create their own poetic identity, on the other hand their primary yardstick for having "made it" resided in critical approval from the very writers they were trying to advance beyond. Like many writers of their generation, Lowell, Olson, and Ginsberg each actively sought a literary mentor, and they modeled their early work on that of their mentor's.

3. *From Modern to Contemporary: American Poetry, 1945–1965*, 2. Breslin's book is the best account of the "anxiety of influence," to use Harold Bloom's term, experienced by post–World War II poets.

4. Lowell, "For John Berryman," 3–4; Ginsberg, July 6, 1955, entry in "Notebooks, 1953–1956"; Charles Olson, *Charles Olson and Ezra Pound: An Encounter at St. Elizabeths*, xxiv.

For instance, in the summer of 1937, Lowell, an unknown at the time, showed up at Tate's Tennessee residence, Benfolly, completely unannounced, pitched a tent on the lawn, and stayed for three months. That summer Lowell, the Tates (Allen and the novelist Caroline Gordon), and another guest at Benfolly, Ford Madox Ford, drove to Olivet College, where Lowell and another poetic fledgling, Theodore Roethke, were students in Tate's sessions at a writers' conference. Lowell recalls that he "altered his style from brilliant free verse" and "became converted to formalism . . . all in two months."[5] Lowell later left Harvard at Tate's suggestion to study at Kenyon under John Crowe Ransom. Eliot, Pound, and Frost, as well as Tate and Ransom, touted his early work. Years later, when Lowell showed Tate the manuscript of *Life Studies,* his first full attempt to move away from New Critical poetry, Tate was appalled, and cautioned Lowell against publishing the work.[6]

Like Lowell, Olson visited Pound at St. Elizabeths Hospital. Lowell's relationship with Pound was a casual one, but Olson conferred with Pound constantly for over two years during the late forties, and he considered Pound his "master." In "ABCs," which takes its title from Pound's primer, *ABC of Reading,* and foreshadows Olson's influential theories in "Projective Verse," Olson acknowledges his debt to Pound at Eliot's expense:

> Style, est verbum
> The word
> is image, and the reverend reverse is Eliot
>
> Pound is verse

In 1948 Olson wrote, "It is a mere son I've been till now," and only after ceasing his visits and renouncing Pound, whose antidemocratic political sentiments and elitist conception of poetry always troubled Olson, did he begin writing "his-story" in the *Maximus Poems.*[7]

Though *Howl and Other Poems* was Ginsberg's first volume to be published, his poetry from the forties, later collected as *The Gates of*

---

5. "The Art of Poetry," 32, and "Visiting the Tates," 557–59.
6. Steven Gould Axelrod, *Robert Lowell: Life and Art,* 92.
7. Sherman Paul, *Olson's Push: Origin, Black Mountain, and Recent American Poetry,* 2–41.

Wrath, was formal, highly stylized—the poems were cast in traditional forms like the sonnet and terza rima—allusive, and full of overblown diction. During this period Ginsberg's poetry reflected New Criticism's emphasis on form because, as he told me in the fall of 1983, "in the forties Auden, Tate, and Eliot *were* poetry." And in *Allen Ginsberg in America* he is quoted as saying that while he was an undergraduate at Columbia in the late forties, "John Crowe Ransom and Allen Tate were like the supreme literary touchstones," and visionary poets such as Whitman and Shelley were considered "creeps."[8] However, in the summer of 1948 Ginsberg's lover, Neal Cassady, abandoned him, and soon after Ginsberg claimed he had experienced an auditory hallucination while masturbating as he read William Blake. In 1949 Ginsberg related this incident and a subsequent hallucination to a psychiatrist, and he was committed to the Columbia Psychiatric Institute. After his release he returned to his hometown of Paterson, New Jersey, where he looked up William Carlos Williams, whom he had met and corresponded with years earlier. In *Allen Verbatim* Ginsberg recalled listening to Williams read "The Cloud" at the Museum of Modern Art and feeling "the whole process" of a "natural prose poetry style" become "immediately clarified."[9] Williams's advice, and his conception of poetry, especially in respect to the use of personal journals, pointed Ginsberg toward the poetics of *Howl and Other Poems,* to which Williams wrote the introduction. Ginsberg's epigraph to his *Collected Poems, 1947–1980* reflects the continued influence of Williams on Ginsberg: "Things are symbols of themselves."

Anecdotes detailing such personal relationships between contemporary and modernist poets could be extended vastly, due in part to the fact that many of the established poets became university teachers, and the younger poets sought them out and became their students. But compared to other poets who broke with modernism in the fifties, Dickey lived in a literary void. Lowell, Olson, Ginsberg, and other poets who emerged as important voices after World War II could afford to wonder if they were destined to become the "uncomfortable epigoni" of the modernists because they

8. Jane Kramer, *Allen Ginsberg in America,* 119.
9. *Allen Verbatim: Lectures on Poetry, Politics, Consciousness,* 144–45.

had established relationships with the older poets and seen their own work published. Dickey, meanwhile, was trying to get his work published through unsolicited manuscripts.

When he entered Vanderbilt as a twenty-three year old in 1946, he was a full-grown man, soon to be married, who had just participated in some of the most horrifying spectacles in human history, but he was still a literary novice. Though Dickey had experienced success in combat duty, earning a Silver Star and two Distinguished Flying crosses in his eighty-seven missions as an airplane navigator and pilot, gone on at Vanderbilt to win the Tennessee state high hurdles championship, and graduated magna cum laude and Phi Beta Kappa in 1949, his career as a writer was still uncertain. When he entered graduate school in 1949 he had yet to publish a poem anywhere other than the campus student magazine, the *Gadfly*, and had achieved little to distinguish him from other graduate students besides his war and athletic experiences; he went through college "gradually building up a belief in [himself] as a writer" (*SI*, 29).

Unlike the poets who fit into the now familiar "mentor-disciple" paradigm, Dickey spurned identification with any immediate literary model. In *Sorties* he claimed that he "could never be part of any literary movement or group" (74), and throughout his career he has maintained this attitude, trenchantly rejecting association with other writers and distancing himself from movements he finds acceptable, such as the agrarian, as well as those he finds contemptible, such as the confessional. Though Dickey has named Malcom Lowry and James Agee as modern figures who served as influences on him, he is quick to state that he admires "their attitude towards experience . . . more than anything they wrote."[10]

In his effort to create an image unique among American poets, he has consciously created a public identity much different from that of other southern writers who emerged from Vanderbilt University. Unlike the gentlemanly cavalier images of Allen Tate, John Crowe Ransom, Robert Penn Warren, and Randall Jarrell, Dickey—the son of a suburban Atlanta lawyer—projects himself as a "good old boy." Nonetheless, Dickey is clearly not a typical good old boy: he graduated with top academic honors from Vanderbilt as an undergradu-

10. Quoted in David Leslie Arnett, "James Dickey: Poetry and Fiction," 119.

ate and graduate student; he knows several languages, has lived in Europe, and has translated a good deal of poetry into English; he has over thirty-five years of experience as a university professor, has written several books of literary criticism, and has won numerous prestigious awards, including the National Book Award, *Poetry*'s Union League Civic and Arts Foundation Prize and its Levinson Award, a Guggenheim Fellowship, the Melville Cane Award, the Longview Foundation Prize, the Vachel Lindsay Award, and two *Sewanee Review* fellowships; he has twice been named Consultant in Poetry to the Library of Congress, was elected to the American Academy of Arts and Letters, and was selected to read at President Carter's inauguration; he has written three novels and several screenplays, and he has acted in films.

Though learned and cosmopolitan, Dickey, who worked as a successful advertising executive, chose to market another image of himself: the decorated combat pilot, track and football star, and outdoors man; the hard-drinking, virile, guitar-playing poet. Through his public image, as well as his verse, Dickey, like Allen Ginsberg, though in a completely different manner, combats the elitist poetry T. S. Eliot advocated. When Dickey writes or comments on his drinking, sexual affairs, musical or athletic interests, he is consciously creating the image of a romantic, earthy, physical, fiercely independent contemporary poet—an image very different from a modernist like Eliot, who was perceived as cerebral, effete, cultured, genteel, and aloof. Dickey's nonfictional prose demonstrates how conscious his attempts to define a literary role for himself have been. Ostensibly, many of these works are simply collections of literary criticism, interviews, and essays, but analysis of these pieces shows how they have been carefully crafted to project an image that repudiates the image of the impersonal poet that the modernists established.

For instance, in the preface to *Self-Interviews* (1970)—the product of Dickey spending several sessions speaking into a tape recorder— the editors mock modernist poets' "impersonal" stance, which they claim is motivated by fear of the "dreaded intentional fallacy," and praise the way Dickey "has openly—courageously—committed himself to . . . looking at his life and work" (9–10). They go on to assert that the book represents a "new genre . . . highly conducive to . . . frankness and honesty" because it "preserves the uninterrupted flow of a poet's spoken words about his life and poetry" (11). Similarly, in the preface to *Night Hurdling* (1983), Dickey discounts Eliot's idea of the poet's "impersonal" nature, and he agrees with "Wallace Stevens, when he says that the impress of a personality is the important quality in poetry" (ix). Indeed, Dickey's poetic device of the "creative lie" closely parallels his "image creating" aesthetic. In "The Self as Agent" Dickey discusses the creative lie as a literary technique:

> The I-figures' actions and meanings, and indeed his very being, are determined by the poet's rational or instinctive grasp of the dramatic possibilities in the scene or situation into which he has placed himself as one of the elements. To put it another way, he sees the creative possibilities of the lie. He comes to understand that he is not after the "truth" at all but something that he considers better. He understands that he is not trying to tell the truth but to *make* it, so that the vision of the poem will impose itself on the reader as more memorable and value-laden than the actuality it is taken from. In the work of many a poet, therefore, the most significant creation of the poet is his fictional self. (*S*, 156)

Notice how closely Dickey's observations on the relationship between a writer's work and his identity parallel his characterization of his poetic aesthetic:

> Perhaps in the end the whole possibility of words being able to contain one's identity is illusory; opinions, yes; identity, maybe. Perhaps the whole question of identity itself is illusory. But one must work with such misconceptions for whatever hint of insight—the making of a truth—they may contain: that fragment of existence which could not be seen in any other way and may with great good luck, as in the best poetry, be better than the truth. (*NH*, xi)

Dickey views a writer's identity, like the "fictional self" presented in the writer's art, as a creation, not an objective entity. Like the world a poem evokes through "creative lies," identity can be "made" to become something "better than the truth," something that will make a more profound impact on the audience. Indeed, by emphasizing selected features of his "personality" that relate to the subject matter of his poetry and his literary concerns, Dickey has carefully constructed a poetic identity that is "better than the truth." Dickey acknowledges that he has "self-dramatized myself out of myself, into something else . . . this is better; it can do something" (S, 74).

Dickey sought to "transfigure" his public self into a more representative or "characteristic" self. He created an image that promoted a literary agenda that involved bringing poetry into the lives of people to whom poetry had become inconsequential. Dickey desired to recapture for poetry an "emotional primitivism" (i.e., compelling readers to respond directly and emotionally rather than intellectually) that he felt had been lost under the reign of the elitist, intellectual modernist poets.

Dickey's essay "Barnstorming for Poetry" (1965) illustrates the conscious use of this strategy to create his poetic identity. Though Dickey had already taught at several universities, published three books of poetry, won various prestigious awards—including a Guggenheim Fellowship—and been nominated for the National Book Award for *Helmets* (1964), the experience he portrays in the essay is not glamorous or sophisticated but romantically stoic. The essay describes Dickey's winter trek across the Midwest in buses, airplanes, and cars (at one point hitchhiking), going from campus to campus reading his poetry. His choice of small midwestern colleges reflects his desire to project himself as a poet of the common man, not an intellectual elite. Moreover, his decision to write about himself in the third person suggests that he is examining a self different from his day-to-day personality.

In the essay Dickey describes himself as a typical "middle-aged" man, "beginning to lose his teeth and hair . . . ordinarily mild-mannered and agreeable," who "secretly thinks of himself as rather colorless and uninteresting." He expresses surprise and gratefulness at the "excessive and even manic" responses with which the audiences greet his readings, declaring that he "has never been lionized by anyone, not even his immediate family; but these small, repeated tastes of local notoriety are definitely agreeable, and he does his best to live up to them." Dickey then addresses the aesthetic of creating the self:

> That, in fact, is his problem: the living up to, the giving them what they want, or might be expected to feel entitled to from a poet

aside from the poems themselves. "Just be yourself," he told himself in the beginning. Ah, but what self? The self he has become on this trip bears but little relation to the self he left at home in the mind, say, of his wife. He has taken to doing some curious things. For example, he has acquired a guitar, which he carries about with him as though he were Carl Sandberg. . . . But it is he who is not satisfied with *just* reading; it is not only poetry that is involved: it is the poet as well. ("BP," 250)

In order to fuse poet and poem, Dickey continues role-playing, purposefully drinking too much and engaging in bizarre antics until one evening before a reading he notices a skull on a table in his room: "Suddenly, at the sight of this *memento mori,* the great themes of poetry hit him squarely: the possibility of love and the inevitability of death." He proceeds to give "the best reading of his life," and he "realizes that all the role-playing is shameful beside the feeling he experiences now." At this point, the process of "transfiguring" the self into a "deeper" self is complete. The "ordinary" middle-aged man has *become* the dynamic poet, and at the end of the tour he asks himself, "Intensity, where have you been all my life?"

The entire essay, as Dickey's use of the third person indicates, is a carefully crafted performance, complete with an epiphany. His presentation of his "usual self" is just as calculated as his creation of a "touring self." Dickey includes biographical details like his age, and mentions life at home and being married, but does not bring up details that would distinguish him from the common person, such as his combat, athletic, and academic records. Dickey comes across as an "average" person *and* a romantic, dynamic poet. In doing so, he stands out as an example of how poetry can be important in the average person's life. Yet even the essay's original place of publication—the first page of the *New York Times Book Review*—betrays his common-man stance as a pose. The essay seems to be about creating a public persona while, in fact, "Barnstorming for Poetry" is a creative lie *projecting* an image that would appeal to the middle-class audience he was trying to reach.

Dickey's five prose collections use a similar approach. Each book's contents, including the books of literary criticism, are not solely presented to enrich the reader's understanding of other writers or literature in general. Like "Barnstorming for Poetry," these books are designed to project and create Dickey's literary identity. His first collection of prose, *The Suspect in Poetry* (1964), is a good example. The bulk of the book consists of previously published two-to-three-page poetry reviews. While the reviews are not thorough or objective, Dickey's strong tone leaves the reader with a deep impression of Dickey's own tastes, positions, and, by implication, poetic practices.

The book fulfilled the exact function Dickey's career needed at that particular stage. When *The Suspect in Poetry* was released, Dickey was still relatively unknown. Reviewers had been generally positive about *Into the Stone and Other Poems* (1960) and *Drowning with Others* (1962), but it was not until 1964 and the release of *The Suspect in Poetry, Helmets,* and *Two Poems of the Air* that Dickey achieved prominence. *The Suspect in Poetry* let readers identify a strong poetic personality with the two new volumes of poetry. Dickey used his critical work to confirm that *Helmets* and *Two Poems of the Air* were the testimony of an intrepid new writer.

Dickey's persistent desire to shun being perceived as an intellectual, while still retaining the reputation of an uncompromising craftsman, is evident in this first prose collection. His method of organizing *The Suspect in Poetry* suggests how he managed to perform this balancing act. In the book Dickey classifies poets into three different categories: "Suspects" (Yvor Winters, Allen Ginsberg, Thom Gunn, Ned O'Gorman, Robert Mezey, Charles Olson, Harold Witt, Anne Sexton, Philip Booth); "Poets of the Second Birth" (Theodore Roethke, Kenneth Patchen, Howard Nemerov, Hayden Carruth, Randall Jarrell, e.e. cummings, Elder Olson, Richard Eberhart, Brother Antoninus); and poets who move "Towards a Solitary Joy" (Gary Snyder, Galway Kinnell, John Logan, W. S. Merwin, William Stafford, David Ignatow).

These groupings are designed not only to reveal Dickey's opinions concerning the status of his contemporaries, but also to suggest Dickey's own status. Given his three categories of poets, the implicit question the book asks and answers is, Where does Dickey fit in? On the book's first page Dickey quickly establishes where he does not fit. Dickey assumes the stance of an angry, disgusted writer, responding to a crisis in contemporary poetry, who desires to make poetry relevant to the common person by ridding it of pretension:

> Most of our contemporary poets are writing out into a climate of
> poetic officialdom, or of pre-tested approval, based largely on the
> principles which the New Criticism has espoused, and on the
> opinions of those who count in modern letters. We have lost all
> sense of personal intimacy between the poet and his reader, and
> even between the poet and his non-poetical self, the self that eats,
> walks down the street, fills out forms, pays taxes, not as a poet,
> but in the same way everybody else does. (9)

Dickey goes on to assert that poetry has become an "effrontery"
to the reader's sense of truth and reality. He maintains that a writer
must stress a "fundamental kind of unliterary innocence" to evoke
real emotions, and that art only "justifies itself" when the reader is
able to forget that his emotions are being "deliberately evoked."
Dickey rejects the "remarkable amount of utter humbug, absolutely
and uselessly far-fetched and complex manipulation of language"
that he perceives on the contemporary scene (9).

In the first section, Dickey complains about Eliot's influence on
poetry by pointing to Eliot's dictum that art is autotelic, and to tech-
niques like those encouraged by Eliot's description of the objective
correlative, as having resulted in a poetry that "comes to seem a
manipulation, much in the same way that advertising or any other
form of propaganda is." Dickey insists poetry has become "suspect,"
and he blames the form's current air of contrivance and artificiality
for this condition and for contributing to the "fatal and much de-
plored rift between poet and audience in our time." Dickey acknowl-
edges that a more subjective and visceral type of poetry and criticism
may seem like "critical chaos" to some, but he regards such a situa-
tion as healthy because "what matters is that there be some real
response to poems, some passionate and private feeling about them."
Dickey calls for poetry and criticism through which the reader gains
"a new, intimate, and vital perspective on his own life as a human
being," and for the end of verse "written by a collective entity called
'Modern Poetry, Period 1945–1960.'" Here, Dickey, who in Self-
Interviews would state that his early poetry was "influenced stylis-
tically . . . by an amalgam of writers: something called, in capital
letters, MODERN POETRY," is doing more than just making a decla-
ration of the direction he believes poetry should take: he is also
asserting the direction his poetry already has taken (SP, 9–11; SI, 46).

During the late fifties and into the sixties Dickey moved away from highly allusive, stylized poetry to verse written in simple language with an unobtrusive, yet controlled, anapestic meter. In much the same way that Dickey strove to project the unassuming image of the common man, he desired poetry that appeared to possess a "fundamental unliterary innocence." He did not so much object to poetry being "manipulative" as to poetry that was obviously manipulative, so that readers realized their emotions were being "deliberately evoked."

Similarly, in his section "Suspects," Dickey manages implicitly to evoke his own aesthetic by juxtaposing Winters and Ginsberg as the two unsatisfactory extremes. Dickey discusses his first "suspect," Winters, indirectly. Instead of commenting on Winters's own poetry, in a section he calls "The Winters Approach" Dickey focuses on a writer whom he considers one of Winters's best pupils, Donald Drummond, and a writer whom he considers one of Winters's worst pupils, Ellen Kay. In selecting this format Dickey not only indicts Winters as a poet, but also demonstrates the pernicious influence of both Winters and the New Criticism: they had spawned a school of automaton poets whose poetry was a meaningless academic exercise.

Dickey acknowledges that Drummond's poems are "thoughtful, cleanly conceived and executed," demonstrate "almost a control-beyond-control of their material," and "have a great deal of compression, intelligence, and wit," yet he finds Drummond "a completely unsatisfactory poet." Dickey goes on to complain that Drummond is a "minor artisan in words," who, like other "Winters-trained writers" has "assimilated entirely, and have put to extremely effective use, the well-known principles and techniques upon which Winters insists with his characteristic air of finality," resulting in poems that are "denatured, dry," and of no "permanent value." Citing William James's claim that "the deeper features of reality are found only in perpetual experience," Dickey writes that Drummond's "lack of physical concreteness" results in verse where a "calculated bleaching process has taken place, wherein life is reduced to a colorless abstraction of itself." Dickey concludes by advising Drummond to read Shakespeare and "even wade shamelessly about in sentimentality" so he can be "enlisted on the side of humanity, rather than that of the Angels" (12–14).

Compared to Ellen Kay, Drummond is treated kindly. Kay "is an almost frightening example of all the worst faults . . . of the average Winters-trained poet, primly preaching academic homilies, wherein painfully-contrived arguments in rhyme substitute for genuine insight." Dickey laments a conception of poetry where "nature is never itself," a conception that chooses "Pluto, Ceres, Eve, the unicorn, Tiresias, The Living Narcissus and, no less wonderful in the pantheon of West-coast neo-classicism, One Intent upon the Doctorate" as its subject matter. Dickey calls such verse essentially "subjectless, all 'strategy' and no passion, all will-power and no luck" (14–15).

Given Dickey's complaints about formulaic and academic poetry, one might suppose that he would have given his sympathy, if not outright support, to a poet like Ginsberg, who shared many of his objections and who was publishing verse that was blatantly unacademic, freer, and unpretentious. However, Dickey sees Ginsberg as "the perfect inhabitant, if not the very founder of Babel, where conditions do not so much make tongues incomprehensible, but render their utterances, as poetry, meaningless." What bothers Dickey about Ginsberg is that Dickey detects no "measure of craft" in his work, and that what emerges from such work is just another example of formulaic verse, in which people with no poetic talent begin to use words like "'strange,' 'mad,' 'angelic,' 'apocalyptic,'—and lo! the neophyte is revealed as a full-blown Ginsbergian or beatnik poet, qualified to read in coffee houses, wear a beard and serve as a 'living symbol' of protest and freedom." Yet Dickey expresses the hope that out of some small publishing house will arise a poet who will "supply the in-touch-with-living authenticity which current American poetry so badly needs" (16–19).

Reminiscent of Whitman's preface to *Leaves of Grass,* Dickey's essay on Ginsberg calls out for himself and promotes the type of poetry he was writing: poetry that is "in-touch-with-living" and retains a measure of form. Like Ginsberg and the Winters-trained poets, all of Dickey's "suspects" fall short either as craftsmen or by emphasizing form and learnedness to the extent that their poetry "lies too much" (10). Besides attacking the New Critics and the beats, Dickey uses the section "Suspects" to mow down representatives of other poetic movements. He admits that Charles Olson has some talent but discounts the originality of Olson's "projective verse," asserting that Olson and his followers simply provide "creative irresponsibility with the semblance of a rationale which may be defended in heated and cloudy terms by its practitioners" (29). He calls Anne Sextons's poetry "very little more than a terribly serious and determinedly outspoken soap-opera," and he charges that "the confessional quality in much recent verse, of which the works of Robert Lowell and W. D. Snodgrass are also cases in point, is giving rise to a new kind of orthodoxy as tedious as the garden-and-picture-gallery school of the forties and fifties" (35).

Dickey's two other categories, "Poets of the Second Birth" and those who move "Towards a Solitary Joy," are presented as palatable alternatives to the "suspects." Dickey reserves his greatest praise for the "poets of the second birth" because such poets combine an original and vital quality of expression with artistic skill. Dickey defines these poets, as opposed to "natural poets like Dylan Thomas," as those who through "the hardest kind of work, much luck, much self-doubt, many false starts, and the difficult and ultimately moral habit of trying each poem, each line, each word, against the shifting but finally constant standard of inner necessity" make themselves poets. Such a poet "must be eternally and ruthlessly vigilant against claiming what is not really his: against fastening on a good Audenesque or Empsonian line, say, and using it because it occurred to him instead of to Auden or Empson." Finally, if the poet endures and is lucky enough to discover his own style, "he will have obliterated or reduced to unimportance the standing distinction between the 'born' poet and the 'made' poet" (55–57).

It is interesting to observe how closely Dickey's definition parallels his own plight as a writer. The essay "The Second Birth" (which was later published in *The Suspect in Poetry*) and Dickey's first successful poems appeared in 1958, when, after over a decade of struggle, his thoughts concerning the state of contemporary poetry and the direction in which he believed poetry and his own career should go had begun to jell. The aesthetic he had started to discover paid off in a series of poems that won the Union League Civic and Arts Foundation Prize from *Poetry* as the best poems submitted to the magazine in 1958 (the year Lowell's *Life Studies* appeared). Consistent with his characterization of "The Second Birth," Dickey did spend years persistently working at his craft despite the fact that his age and background were against him. Dickey did experience many "false starts," and he did have to work through the process of finally rejecting the poetic style of prominent poets before discovering a style that fit his own sensibility.

This oblique act of self-definition can be viewed both as the projection of a wish to render inconsequential the difference between "natural" poets and "made" poets like himself, and of the assertion of that wish coming true for Dickey. That critics commonly call Dickey a poet of the "Second Birth," though Dickey never refers to himself in this manner, indicates just how effectively such a tactic has worked. *The Suspect in Poetry* and Dickey's other collections of prose are not brilliant works of literary criticism, but effective performances in the art of creating a public image. Dickey's comments on other writers and literary matters are often insightful but always colorful and brazen—putting the focus on himself rather than on his ostensible subject. He is anything but "objective" and "impersonal."

The public image he has projected has served him well and sometimes spectacularly among a general readership; however, as I will later show, his "good old boy" image eventually backfired among academic critics, who began to equate Dickey's image with various personae used in his poems. Nevertheless, he has created a poetic self that sharply contrasts with the image of the modernists and of his contemporaries. Most important, understanding the development of Dickey's image is essential to comprehending fully his poetic aesthetic and the literary mission he set for himself. Discussing the purpose behind Dickey's public personality provides a microcosm of his career—his goals, concerns, and practices—for Dickey's poetry consistently addresses the transformation of self, and the sensual, aggressive, anti-intellectual qualities that characterize the Dickey image are vital components of the transformed, "energized" self he seeks and voices in his poems.

In the following chapters I turn to the development of Dickey's aesthetic and its cultural and political implications. As will become evident in the next chapter, the antimodernist stance of Dickey's image is in some ways misleading. Dickey tried to be a modernist before he set himself in opposition to his immediate predecessors, and, as I will demonstrate, his early aesthetic owes a debt to Ezra Pound's conception of the poetic image.

1

The Uncollected Dickey
New Criticism, Pound, and
the Narrative Image

In the late forties and early fifties James Dickey was
trying to get his work published by submitting unsolicited manu-
scripts. Dickey recalled later that while he was at Vanderbilt from
1947 to 1950 he would "go into the stacks of the library and get a
magazine out . . . and get the address off the masthead and send the
poem to the guy who was the editor at that address. . . . I could have
papered my bedroom wall with the rejections."[1] Indeed, Dickey's
career as poet began like those of many others—with many rejec-
tions and a few acceptances. What Dickey needed to discover dur-
ing the fifties was the proper poetic form to fit his temperament, his
subject matter, and the public image of himself he was beginning to
establish. Hence much of his early work was written in a variety of

---

1. "James Dickey," interview in *Writers at Work: The Paris Review Interviews,* ed.
George Plimpton, 202.

styles. Critics have disregarded or been unaware of this phase of Dickey's development; instead, they have chosen to treat Dickey's first volume, *Into the Stone and Other Poems*, as the start of his career, ignoring the still uncollected poems Dickey published throughout the fifties in prestigious journals such as *Poetry*, the *Sewanee Review*, the *Hudson Review*, and the *Yale Review*, long before *Into the Stone*'s publication in 1960.[2]

Two factors have helped create this omission. First, interest in Dickey's colorful biography, especially his well-documented war, athletic, and business experiences, has overshadowed his early work. The popular Dickey legend of a middle-aged ex-combat pilot and ex-athletic star who turned his back on a lucrative business career suddenly to become a successful poet makes good copy.

Second, Dickey's manner of marketing his work has turned attention away from his poetry published before 1957. Dickey has occasionally referred to this part of his career in interviews, and he has even issued a limited number of highly priced collectors' editions of some of these poems, but critics continue to know his early work through *Poems, 1957–1967* and *The Early Motion* (1981), the latter a collection containing *Drowning with Others* and *Helmets*, his second and third books. Though *The Whole Motion*, Dickey's collected poems, includes previously unpublished early verse, it does not contain any uncollected poems that were published in the fifties. The four collections of essays on Dickey and the three other books on his career—Richard Calhoun and Robert W. Hill's *James Dickey* (1983), Ronald Baughman's *Understanding James Dickey* (1985), and Robert Kirschten's *James Dickey and the Gentle Ecstasy of Earth* (1988)—demonstrate the effect of such marketing: not a single poem published before "The Father's Body" in December 1956 is mentioned in any of these studies. This omission is all the more startling when one considers that Calhoun and Hill's book and the collection of essays Harold Bloom edited,

2. Fred Walker Robbins, in "The Poetry of James Dickey, 1951–1967," does address Dickey's early uncollected poems; however, Robbins's consideration of the poetry goes little beyond close readings, and he does not view the material in the context of New Criticism, modernism, and the post–World War II literary milieu. Because of the purposes of my study, I am not so much interested in what Dickey's early poems "mean," but in what these poems reveal about Dickey's relationship to New Criticism and modernism.

James Dickey: Modern Critical Views (1987), look at Dickey's career chronologically in an effort to trace his development as a writer.

The twenty-one still uncollected poems Dickey published between 1951 and 1957 (he has not collected any poems that appeared before 1957) show that Dickey was trying to write poetry that conformed to modernist and New Critical standards. By 1957, the same year Dickey broke off his correspondence with Ezra Pound, he had taken what he could use from Pound and opted to write in the romantic visionary mode characteristic of Dickey's best work. His early uncollected poems and his correspondence with Pound demonstrate Dickey's struggle to move out from under modernism's domination and arrive at his poetic point d'appui through the development of an image-centered poetry that would accommodate his romantic sensibility and his affection for narrative forms.[3]

Dickey's decision after returning from combat duty in the Pacific theater to attend a university with such a strong New Critical emphasis as Vanderbilt undoubtedly helped shape his early poetry. There, Dickey formed a profound and lasting relationship with one of his professors, Monroe Spears. Dickey took two of Spears's courses, including a class in eighteenth-century poetry, talked with him at length over several years, and, under his guidance, began experimenting with traditional genres, like verse satire, and traditional forms, such as the couplet.[4] Though Spears helped Dickey in many ways, some of the poems Dickey wrote under his influence were nothing short of disastrous. The poem "Of Holy War" (1951) is a good example:

> O sire, I dreamed
> You danced with greaves
> Afire (it seemed)

3. I apply the word *romantic* (using lowercase to avoid the danger of seeming monolithic) to Dickey as Rene Wellek defined it in *Concepts of Criticism*: a writer's ability to "see the implication of imagination, symbol, myth and organic nature and see it as part of the great endeavor to overcome the split between subject and object, the self and the world, the conscious and the unconscious" (220). In turning toward a romantic mode of expression, Dickey rejected the New Critics' emphasis on the impersonal nature of the artist, their embracing of formal restraint and an objective theory of art, their sense of alienation and despair, their disdain for doctrines of self-expression and self-perfectibility, and their emphasis on irony and ambiguity.

4. Interviews with author, August 8–15, 1989.

At Acre, or leaves
In Caen gave on
A peregrine:
Coal under plume
Penumbrally seen.

That phoenix watched.
Rood and gate
Embered and percht
His spread weight.
Sire flee this shadow.
I grass his meadow.

For a variety of reasons, it is difficult to believe that Dickey, whose best work relies on simple diction with a narrative, anecdotal element, wrote this poem. The inflated language in phrases such as "Penumbrally seen," the allusions to Bunyan's *The Holy War* and perhaps Yeats ("Rood") and Lawrence ("phoenix"), and the archaic spelling ("percht") remind one of the self-conscious academic poetry Dickey would denounce six years later in his essay "From Babel to Byzantium." In "Of Holy War" Dickey juxtaposes the holy war at Acre, the scene of much fighting during the Christian Crusades in the twelfth and thirteenth centuries, and the modern holy war at Caen, the city in Normandy that was a primary target of the allied invasion in World War II. Though the subject matter of war would remain a typical theme in Dickey's work, his use of a spare, allusive form here is an awkward and revealing example of the verse he was trying to write during the late forties and early fifties.

Despite the evident weakness of this poem, *Poetry* accepted "Of Holy War" because it conformed, if only superficially, to the standards the New Critical community was advocating. Except for lines two and four of the second stanza, which use a three-syllable, three-stress beat, Dickey uses four syllables and three stresses per line. A strong end rhyme is forced (the phrase "it seemed" is otherwise unnecessary) through the parenthetical interjection in line three. The poem's deference to tradition and emphasis on form flattered the sensibilities of a literary community whose biases had been shaped largely by the impersonal, objective, intellectual verse advocated by Eliot in his essays, and in influential texts such as Warren and Brooks's *Understanding Poetry*.

In *Self-Interviews* Dickey recalled that his early poetry was "influenced stylistically not so much by individual writers as by an amalgam of writers: something called, in capital letters, MODERN POETRY. I wanted to make it sound like 'modern poetry' and not like Stevens or Thomas" (46). For Dickey this meant trying to curb his own natural predilection for sensuous, energetic, romantic verse in an attempt to be published more widely. After all, Wallace Stevens was viewed as a sort of anomaly, and the robust romantic verse of Dylan Thomas, with its pagan sense of the elemental, had never been completely accepted by Pound, T. S. Eliot, W. H. Auden, or Allen Tate. In 1947 Robert Lowell, who by this time had won the Pulitzer Prize for *Lord Weary's Castle* and been highly acclaimed by the New Critics, wrote, "If Thomas kept his eye on the object and depended less on his rhetoric, his poems would be better organized and have more to say." Lowell considered Tate "somehow more of a model" than Thomas or Hart Crane because he had both "wildness" and "construction."[5] By insisting that Thomas "keep his eye on the object" and depend less on "rhetoric," Lowell was advocating the New Critical preference for imagistic, dramatic verse. He suggested that while Thomas was merely windy, Tate's poetry contained energy and form. Lowell's statements indicate the type of poetry that the New Critical community did advocate: a poetics that stressed craftsmanship and objectivity and was intellectual ("have more to say") rather than emotive.

Such biases had become so strong that to many young poets—Dickey among them—it seemed essential that they conform to New Critical standards while still appearing innovative enough to merit attention. The raison d'être given by a little magazine in the fall of 1950 indicates just how suffocating this environment had become: on the first page of its initial issue the editors of the *Beloit Poetry Journal* declared that while most little poetry magazines had become too "specialized," especially *Poetry*, with its affinity for "learned" aspects of the craft, their magazine hoped "to provide a varied diet for the reader whose first loyalty is to good poetry, regardless of whether it conforms to the formulae of the New Criticism or not."

"The Shark in the Window," published in the *Sewanee Review*

5. "Thomas, Bishop, and Williams," 493, and "Art of Poetry," 28–29.

(1951), further demonstrates Dickey's eagerness to imitate New Critical poetics. Dickey wrote the poem as a tribute to his brother's marriage; during the drive home in the fog after his brother's wedding, the narrator remembers a moment when he and his brother were staring at a shark through an aquarium window and experienced a feeling of oneness with the shark and with each other. Though the exact nature of the feeling is never clear, the narrator concludes the poem by wishing that his brother and sister-in-law might come to know a similar union of spirit.

As in "Of Holy War," the diction of "The Shark in the Window" is pretentious, and Dickey's attempt at philosophical depth only achieves nonsensical obscurity. In places the poem becomes incomprehensible:

> We enter to find ourselves the same in love,
> In kinship, as the tussled cloth about
> A river-reed's needle, a stitching snag, can
> Never alter, but renders Platonist and Caddis
> Fly the selfsame cordonnet, as of point-laced, ancient,
> Vital hair, though the water move
> More calmly than the waters of a grape, or mull
> Sienna-spread and vastly wild
> Under ephemarae of mule and leaf.

Dickey's point is simple—he and his brother are as one—but his reference to the "Platonist" and "Caddis / Fly" is unclear. The reader never knows if Dickey is drawing an analogy between himself and his brother, and the Platonist and the fly, or even how the line relates to the remainder of the poem. References such as the "ephemarae of mule and leaf" are gratuitous, having no connection to the rest of the poem. Dickey seems to be trying to make some point about the permanent and the transitory in a philosophically abstract manner reminiscent of Eliot, Yeats, and Tate, but the idea is not taken up again, nor is it made clear how it relates to what Dickey is saying about himself and his brother. Where in his maturer poetry Dickey aims for simplicity and lucidity, in his early verse he wanted to appear learned and complex. As a result many of his early poems are pretentious and opaque.

Two poems that appeared in *Poetry* (1953), "The Child in Armor" and "The Anniversary," further reveal the aesthetic norms Dickey was aspiring to meet. Though these poems are grouped together under the heading "Two Poems," the dissimilarities between them are more telling than their similarities. In "The Anniversary" Dickey tries on Eliot's mantle, which he later rejected. "The Anniversary" is written in a style meant to resemble that of Donne, whom the New Critics, especially Eliot, in his well-known essay "The Metaphysical Poets," had praised.

The poem's title alludes to Donne's sonnet "The Anniversarie," in which the narrator claims that though a year has passed and all things of the world have aged and are closer "to their destruction drawn," his and his lady's "love hath no decay." Dickey's poem is an ironic reversal of Donne's: the poem details a pleasant, soothing sexual experience that later goes awry. Dickey splits the poem in two parts: the first part deals with both the positive sexual experience and alchemy, a motif Donne often used, which together form a conceit indicating the complete bodily unification of the two lovers, culminating in

> Two golds together
> That else would've been
> No hue of the scene.

In the second part, Dickey uses the image of the narrator playing a guitar, symbolic of the lover's body, to describe the unsatisfactory experience. The metaphysicals' strong inclination to psychological analysis of the emotions of love and their affection for the novel and shocking ("The hell of the ear, / I splay the guitar, / Bleeding my faces"), rough verse, extremes, obscurity, and strained imagery are all present, though without the accomplished performance of Donne's poem. Indeed, Donne's penchant for the baroque is evident when examing the disparate images—metallurgy, sewing, guitar playing, bookmaking—Dickey uses in the poem.

Written primarily in couplets or by rhyming every other line, the poem's rhymes flow naturally in places:

> Broke clear as hazard
> And perisht hard
> Against the breast

> The sun not help
> Nor moon destroy,
> Left whole the beast
> And bled the boy.

In other instances the verse seems forced and the rhymes sophomoric:

> Warm in such braces,
> Mentioning grasses,
> Grinning disgraces
> And opulent faces.

In contrast, the second poem, "The Child in Armor," is more conversational, more recognizably Dickey, and though the poem's first two stanzas loosely conform to an *a b a b* scheme, the insistence on end rhymes is not as strained, and half rhymes are used effectively (" . . . precise / . . . mace" and " . . . crest / . . . furnished"). More importantly, unlike the "objective" narration of "The Anniversary," "The Child in Armor" is concerned with the aesthetics of perception. The poem, which describes a father's impressionistic fantasy of his young son garbed in armor as the man views the boy playing at a window, typifies Dickey's later work by its focus on the narrator's subjective transformation of an ordinary event at a particular time and place. The manner in which the play of light affects and shapes the narrator's perceptions is strongly akin to the way in which Dickey later handles the play of light in "Armor," "The Dusk of Horses," "The Beholders," and "Dust," all poems written during the sixties.

Despite such an occasional flirtation with subjectivity, during the fifties Dickey predominantly continued to tinker with techniques the modernists had established. The influence of imagism and its variants as practiced by Eliot, Pound, and others can be seen in "The Ground of Killing," which appeared in the *Sewanee Review* in 1954. The poem represents Dickey's first attempt to combine an image-centered technique with a narrative framework, foreshadowing his mature aesthetic. In "The Ground of Killing" Dickey describes a heron diving into the water after a fish:

> The heron's shade
> Black beak for orange.
> Doubles God willed.
> Wind riffles both,
> Water, one.

Dickey meticulously builds image upon image of the bird parting the water and spearing its prey:

> The eye of the heron
> Enters precisely the side
> Of the fish and passes
> Into the red village.

The poem is more successful than Dickey's experiments with older poetic forms because his eye for physical detail and his talent for capturing action through kinetic, driving verse complement the poem's imagistic quality. However, the images in "The Ground of Killing" are presented objectively: the swimmer in the poem, who is attempting to spear a fish with a trident, observes the heron kill the fish, but subjective transformation of the moment into an experience confirming a primitive, tribal self—a cornerstone of Dickey's later work—never occurs.

More examples of Dickey's experimentations with modernist and New Critical forms could be provided, but the poems discussed above make the point clearly enough. Though published within three years of one another, each poem demonstrates a different style, suggesting the aesthetic uncertainty Dickey was feeling. In a letter to Ezra Pound dated February 1956, he lamented that though several of his poems had been published, "I can't for the life of me think they're what I want."[6] Indeed, Dickey spent nearly a decade trying to imitate modernist and New Critical poetics before discovering a suitable style.

Dickey's correspondence with Pound demonstrates his eventual decision to move out from under modernist and New Critical expectations. This bizarre exchange of letters, in which Dickey de-

6. All of the known correspondence between Dickey and Pound is reprinted in Lee Bartlett and Hugh Witemeyer, "Ezra Pound and James Dickey: A Correspondence and a Kinship."

scribes an incident that led him to quit his teaching position at the University of Florida, also illustrates his anxious efforts to forge a literary career.

Like so many other poets of his generation who tried to write "MODERN POETRY," Dickey sought out Pound at St. Elizabeths Hospital in Washington, D.C. The only times Dickey ever met Pound occurred after Dickey had returned from Europe in August 1955, but over the next two years he wrote six letters to Pound, and in turn received six letters and three postcards from him.[7] Lee Bartlett and Hugh Witemeyer have speculated that because Dickey "has never modeled his own poetic style upon that of Pound" he was perhaps "seeking the support of a father from whom he could yet remain independent." However, Dickey's own conception of the image reveals a more profound debt to Pound than these critics suppose, and the letters he exchanged with Pound, as well as his comments in interviews with me, show Dickey's enthusiasm for Pound's poetic theories.

Dickey's first letter demonstrates his desire to ingratiate himself with Pound. Dickey begins the letter, dated August 29, 1955, by telling the older man that he would "very much like to hear from" him, and he goes on to praise Pound, informing him that their

7. After receiving a graduate fellowship at Vanderbilt in 1950 and writing his Master's thesis, "Symbol and Imagery in the Shorter Poems of Herman Melville"—a New Critical reading of Melville's work—Dickey took a teaching job at Rice with the intention of continuing to work on his writing. However, after the fall semester he was recalled by the Air Force to serve in the Korean War. Thus in 1951, at age twenty-eight, with his education recently completed, his first poems just published, his teaching position finally secured, and his wife pregnant with their first child, Dickey, who had "hoped never to be in another plane again," went into combat duty once more. Dickey describes this time as "dreadful" and "traumatic," and he has since remarked that the only thing that "sustained" him through this experience was the acceptance of a few poems by the *Sewanee Review* and *Poetry* (*SI*, 41).

After the war Dickey returned to Rice, but the English department's chairman, Allan McKillop, insisted he pursue the Ph.D. or continue teaching low-level courses in a nontenured position. At the suggestion of Monroe Spears, who was now teaching at Rice and still editing the *Sewanee Review,* a frustrated Dickey applied for a *Sewanee Review* fellowship. Two fellow Vanderbilt alumni, Andrew Lytle and Allen Tate, served as judges for the competition and awarded Dickey the fellowship. Dickey then took his family to Europe in 1954, where he wrote and traveled before returning to the states, and, at Lytle's behest, accepted a position at the University of Florida as Lytle's assistant (*SI*, 42).

meeting had resulted in "a new orientation towards America for me," though he does not specify the nature of the change. Dickey also states that now that "l'annee de la poesie" is over, he is on his way to teach at the University of Florida, and he signs off with "Ave Caesar, morituri te salutant!" and another appeal for Pound to write back.

Dickey's use of Latin, phrases like "l'annee de la poesie," and the letter's general tone show that he was trying to *act* like a modernist— a sharp contrast to Dickey's later "good old boy" image. In the letter Dickey presents a continental sensibility to Pound. He comments on America's cultural bankruptcy, lamenting, "American life has us by the throat again," and "Europe seems very far away and inaccessible, and poetry has come again to have the attributes of a personal weapon rather than those of artisanship."

Pound replied within the week, but most of the letter concerns his search for the address of a mutual friend, Bill Pratt. Dickey's writing, or even his current state of affairs, are never mentioned. Rather than showing irritation over the lack of personal attention, Dickey's reply shows him more intent than ever to endear himself to Pound. Dickey opens his second letter by referring to Pound as "Cher Maitre," and after providing Pratt's address, he announces:

> My wife and I are collaborating on a project (she works, and I goad) to knit you a sweater, or I guess it will be a kind of sweater, though at the present stage it knows more what it is trying to be than we do. Would you like the Gaudier sketch worked in, if we can (we can't guarantee artistry, but can fumble at similarity) work it in? . . . I have written a long, over violent and pretty good poem, which I shall send you after a few more weeks, if you like.

Dickey's gesture worked, as Pound once again responded within a week. Most of Pound's letter has to do with the sweater Dickey promised, including Pound's drawings of how the sweater should be designed. Pound tells Dickey that the notion meets with his "highest commendation," and he asks if Dickey wants his "measurements" for the sweater and the poem. Pound specifies how a sweater and a poem "fer XrizaChe" should be made—"don't make it short . . . OMIT fancy adornments/trouble enuf to git garment

constructed"—and tells Dickey "O.K. send the poEM/." In his next
letter Dickey addresses Pound as "Dear Uncle," thanks him "for the
continued attention," and signs the note with a phrase replete with
Poundian abbreviations: "Yr O'bt Sv't."

In the poem he offered to send Pound, "The Father's Body" (later
published in *Poetry* [1956]), Dickey seems to take Pound's advice by
dealing with his subject matter in a more straightforward manner.
The poem concerns a boy's first impression of the physical differ-
ences between him and his father, and it concludes with the boy's
imaginary first sexual experience with a girl, over which the father
presides. In "The Father's Body" Dickey's earlier gestures of learn-
edness are absent, and he addresses sexuality more boldly than
before. Foreshadowing his later work, Dickey takes a commonplace
event, a father and son showering in a wooden bathhouse after a
swim, and gives it ritualistic, mythic significance. The father takes
on the look "Of ruined, unarrestable statuary / not made by men,"
and the boy becomes aware of his father's nakedness as he steps
into the shower to join him. When the water sprays on the boy's
face, he closes his eyes, entering into an imaginative reverie where
he finds himself and his father engaging in a ritual of creation and
self-discovery. Through his reverie and the image of his father's
body, the boy creates an image of his own completeness and sexual
coming-of-age. In the boy's daydream the father shapes the boy's
physical self, and proceeds to shape the body of a girl so that the
boy can gain a "soul."

The father watches the boy and girl become complete as they
enter into sexual union:

> Above them, his father's eyes are aging
> With the sky, dancing about them
> A pattern swum from wood, watched luminous from silk.
> And he feels his father rise
> Through his own slight, helpless loins
> Into the frankness of space.
> He falls through her from there, and her eyes change.
>
> The shadow of the cross
> Of a sword-hilt held awkwardly by his father
> Imprints itself on his back, floating and burning.
> He parts the girl's terrible legs; he shouts

> Out silence; his waist points
> And holds and points, empowered
> Unbearably; withheld: withheld—
>
> . . . released.

Though Dickey never sent Pound "The Father's Body," he did read the poem to the American Pen Women's Society, a group of faculty wives at the University of Florida, during spring term of the 1955–1956 academic year. According to Dickey the poem caused an uproar, resulting in the university's demand for an apology. Dickey refused, and he claims that he walked out, never to teach at Florida again.

Given the frankness with which Dickey presents sexuality in these stanzas, and the social climate of the South in 1956, he may have intended to outrage his audience. Indeed, after completing his *Sewanee Review* fellowship in Europe, Dickey returned to the states and began to seek notoriety, publishing reviews and essays railing against many contemporary trends in poetry and calling for new, more vital verse. Dickey was unhappy with his work at Florida because rather than teaching creative writing as he was promised, he was assigned to teach freshman composition. Reading the poem before faculty wives, and at a school whose faculty included Andrew Lytle and the poet Gene Baroff, and where writers like Robert Frost and John Ciardi were frequent visitors, Dickey and the poem stood to gain notice before the poem was published.[8] As he told Pound in a letter dated February 20, 1956, dismissal would only result in more publicity while ridding him of a job he did not want. Dickey has often since used this incident in interviews and personal essays to date the *real* start of his career:

> But there was building up in my mind a conviction about how poetry would have to be for me. . . . I had begun to get some notion of the kind of poem I wanted to write. I wanted to do something about sensual experience that had not yet been done.

8. Richard Vowles, who taught at Florida in the 1950s, in a taped interview with me in Madison, Wisconsin, on May 17, 1988, described Gainesville as "the scene of a great deal of creative activity while Dickey was there. Writers like Frost, Ciardi, Jarrell, and a host of other writers and artists were always coming in and out of town."

> So I wrote a poem called "The Father's Body." . . . As a result
> of writing this poem and reading it at the insistence of a group of
> ladies at the University of Florida, I got into a certain amount of
> trouble which I resolved by walking out. I told Andrew Lytle that
> I had no further interest in teaching at the University of Florida—
> which indeed I did not, and I haven't seen him to this day—and I
> told the authorities there I had no intention of apologizing for my
> supposed transgression. (*SI*, 42–43)

Critics often refer to this incident because it makes the perfect
start for the type of legendry associated with Dickey, ignoring the
groping and self-conscious imitation of his early work. In fact, "The
Father's Body" is the only early uncollected poem critics refer to at
all in the eight books on Dickey. This account makes Dickey come
across as an original, independent maverick whose work is so real
and sensuous that stuffy academics and pious ladies could not
accept it.

Dickey's February letter to Pound never mentions "The Father's
Body," and it characterizes the genesis of his problems at Florida
much differently:

> There is not much to say here, except a whole generation of Flor-
> ida students is being brought up on the *ABC of Reading*, much to
> the astonishment of the Cerberi of the English Department. Also, I
> lectured, I mean "lectured," to the American Pen Women's Society
> so furiously (and, I guess controversially) that their National Pres-
> ident wrote to the president of *this* place and demanded that I be
> kicked out. I haven't been, yet, but the U. of Florida may martyr
> me still. I rather hope so, though it may be just possible that I am
> doing one or two people some good here.

In this passage Dickey presents himself as an ally spreading Pound's
gospel. Dickey implies that the "establishment" could not handle
Pound's theories or those Dickey presented in his "lecture." He
suggests that, like Pound, he will also be victimized by an establish-
ment that persecutes progressive-minded men of letters. However,
in the passage from *Self-Interviews* and in other accounts, Dickey
never mentions lecturing, and he indicates that the incident oc-
curred almost by accident, involving nothing more than his reading
of the poem. For example, in a 1982 letter to Lee Bartlett, Dickey
remembers: "I read some poetry to them, none of it mine, and at

their insistence read part of a poem called 'The Father's Body,' which I had in my pocket and was working on. This had some sexual references that the (Pen) Women didn't like, and they made complaint. I refused to apologize and left the University."

Dickey and Pound did not correspond again until August 15, 1956, when Dickey finally mailed the sweater he had promised almost a year earlier. In that letter he also praises Pound's last ten *Cantos* and informs Pound that he "left University of Florida *in medias res,* 'all accusations refuted but that of being the bohemian type.'"

Dickey's standard version of the incident fits the Dickey "legend" that has gained him so much notoriety, while the version he provided Pound met Dickey's desire to gain Pound's respect and attention.[9] Though Dickey never revealed to Pound the contents of his "furious" and "controversial" lecture, Pound, as is evident in his reply, interpreted the incident as a political attack, perhaps because of remarks like Dickey's earlier claim that meeting Pound had resulted in a "new orientation towards America" for Dickey. By calling himself a potential "martyr" in the February letter, Dickey surely struck a note of sympathy with Pound, who viewed himself as a political and literary martyr.

Dickey's desire that Pound consider him a literary comrade worked all too well, because the version of the incident he sent Pound

9. John O. Lyons, who also taught at Florida during Dickey's stay there, and Richard Vowles were not aware that Dickey's early departure had anything to do with his lecturing or reading a poem. Lyons, in an interview with me on May 10, 1988, stated that he was under the impression that, much to Andrew Lytle's chagrin, Dickey departed before the semester ended for a well-paying job in the business sector. According to Lyons, Lytle was "furious" because Dickey had left without grading a stack of his students' papers or turning in final grades. In May 1988 I wrote Lytle inquiring about the incident, but Lytle politely declined to comment.

That Dickey first mentioned the incident to Pound in a letter dated February 20, yet did not leave the University of Florida until April, suggests that his reading "The Father's Body" was perhaps not the only cause for his departure. In April 1956 Dickey took a job with the McCann-Erickson advertising firm in New York, where he worked on the Coca-Cola account. After about a year, Dickey returned to Atlanta to work as senior writer and creative director on the account of the local Coca-Cola bottler, later moving to the firm of Liller, Neal, Battle, and Lindsay to work on a successful advertising campaign for Lay's Potato Chips. Dickey was so successful that in 1959 he was voted "Atlanta's Young Man on the Go" and given a job as creative director for Atlanta's largest advertising agency, Burke, Dowling, Adams, where Dickey managed the Delta Airlines account.

quickly backfired when Pound identified Dickey as a potential as-
sociate in various political causes. In less than a week Pound re-
sponded by thanking Dickey for the sweater, admonishing him for
not keeping in touch, and trying to enlist Dickey's help in battling
the economic conspiracy Pound believed would bring about the
downfall of the Western world. When Dickey, perhaps wary of
what he had begun, did not reply, Pound wrote back, making sev-
eral anti-Semitic remarks ("the Spewiltzers have been engaged in
debasing the coinage of criticism and of American writing in gen-
eral") and urging Dickey that "If yu are sighing for action" he
should enlist in a "super ku klu klux." Pound signed the letter, "yrs
in strict anonymity." Again, Dickey, who had expressed his support
for the civil rights movement in his essay "Notes on the Decline of
Outrage," did not reply.

Dickey found himself in a difficult situation: he wanted to court
Pound's favor, but without committing himself to Pound's fascist
causes. Nine months later, in May 1957, Pound wrote Dickey urging
him to contact the editors of the Australian magazine *Edge*, the
mouthpiece of a white racist group sympathetic to Pound's ideas. In
early June Dickey replied with a letter in which he announced the
"Partisan Review people" had promised to bring out a book of his
poems, and that he would "write the *Edge* people and see what they
have." He also asked Pound to recommend some books on mone-
tary reform. Dickey evaded providing Pound with a direct response
concerning his political sympathies, saying that he "knows nothing
about money except that it is hard to come by." Pound responded to
Dickey's requests within a couple of days with a letter full of viru-
lent anti-Semitic remarks, clearly viewing Dickey as a comrade in
his struggle, and warning him against the leftist *Partisan Review:* "if
Pen Women mean P.E.N. club wimmen / yu have been ditched by
one dirty jew gang to be taken up by another / be prudent and
don't mention my name till the bastards have actually printed you /
but better try a clean outfit / sometimes they cop a work merely to
put it into the cellar."

Dickey apparently never contacted Pound again, though Pound
sent him two postcards, one dated June 23, 1958, and the other
November 7, 1958, asking for some "NOOZ" about what Dickey
was doing. Pound ended the second card with a racist slur, asking

how Dickey felt about living in the South, with "so many dem / cong / men."

For years Dickey was silent about his relationship with Pound, only bringing up his name, usually along with Eliot's, as an example of the kind of elitism that plagued poetry. Even in *Self-Interviews*, where Dickey commented on this period of his career in detail, he never acknowledged knowing Pound. However, since 1975, when in an interview Dickey mentioned corresponding with Pound, he has spoken about Pound's aesthetic at length.[10] In the 1979 Ezra Pound Lecture at the University of Idaho, "The Waterbug's Mittens, Ezra Pound: What We Can Use," later published in *Night Hurdling* (29–46), Dickey "sought to clarify [his] own feelings about Pound's work" and to determine what aspects of Pound's work contained continuing value (29).

In the published lecture, Dickey declares, "What I like in Pound is exactly the opposite of what the literary world has taken him to represent. I like the maker (the *fabbro*) of the clean phrase and the hard edge imaginative image, and am tempted to let most of the rest of Pound go" (37). Though Dickey modifies this statement slightly, praising Pound's imaginative translations and the "strong Anglo-Saxon rhythm" of his verse, he laments the *Cantos'* "lack of actual concern with people. . . . Every person that Pound brings to our attention is an example of something . . . a stand-in for an abstraction" and the "distressing erector-set mechanicalness . . . complex in-group snobbery, [and] very off putting air of contemptuous intellectual superiority" of the work (43). Dickey discovers value in the "surfaces" of Pound's work, such as the image of a water bug on a rock from the *Cantos'* "Section: Rock-Drill," not in the "ill-digested philosophy, economics, history and politics" in which the "Hugh Kenners and Donald Davies of the world, the professors," find "profit" (44).

10. In "James Dickey: Interview" Dickey first commented on knowing Pound personally. Dickey claimed that he visited Pound "a few times" and that they engaged in a "tremendous correspondence." Dickey's characterization seems exaggerated. Only one meeting between Dickey and Pound is mentioned in the correspondence, and none of the twelve letters they exchanged went much over a page in length.

Dickey's statements help define the direction his own career was heading in 1957. What Dickey does take from Pound is the image; he also developed a "strong Anglo-Saxon" rhythm of his own in the anapestic meter that so distinctly marks his poems from 1958 to 1964. Dickey remembers that he read "all of [Pound's essays] many times over and over" in the mid-to-late fifties, and that what he "picked out" from Pound was "an extreme . . . magical directness, which is the ability to take something which is factual and make a simple highly imaginative statement out of it. . . . I like the thing that comes like a lightning flash and that is vivid and unmistakable." But in sharp contrast to Pound's elitism, in the late fifties Dickey started to present himself as a poet of the common man (perhaps his reason for not acknowledging his association with Pound earlier), and he began to simplify his diction while concentrating on developing his use of the image. Dickey began to aim for a "very clear, country-simple, highly original and highly imaginative . . . kind of deep simplicity." Rather than focusing primarily on particular objects, "in things," and using an objective mode of presentation, Dickey began to develop a kind of image-centered technique that I call a *narrative image:* he began to create radically subjective extended images that encompassed an entire event or story. Indeed, Dickey has pointed out that "the image and the dramatic development" became "the guts of it for me."[11]

Dickey's development of the narrative image owes a great deal to Pound's conception of the image. In "A Retrospect" Pound defines the image as "an intellectual and emotional complex in an instant of time." He pronounces, "It is the presentation of such a 'complex' instantaneously which gives that sense of sudden liberation; that sense of freedom from time limits and space limits; that sense of sudden growth," and he advocates the use of concrete images, stripped of adjectival adornments. He predicts that poetry in this century will

> move against poppy-cock, it will be harder and saner, it will be
> what Mr. Hewlett calls 'nearer to the bone.' It will be as much like
> granite as it can be, its force will lie in its truth, its interpretive
> power . . . it will not try to seem forcible by rhetorical din, and

11. "An Interview with James Dickey," 118.

luxurious riot. We will have fewer painted adjectives impeding the shock and stroke of it. At least for myself, I want it so, austere, direct, free from emotional slither.[12]

In an uncollected poem Dickey published about the time he stopped corresponding with Pound, "To Be Edward Thomas," Dickey works out the narrative image's aesthetic, drawing on Pound's definition of the image.[13] The poem demonstrates Dickey's preoccupation with the use of the image and the art of creating poetry—a subject appropriate for Dickey, who was in his mid-thirties and yet only beginning to discover a suitable poetic voice or form. Thus "To Be Edward Thomas" represents a connective pivot between Dickey's awkward modernism and his later successful, innovative poetry; it is Dickey's fullest early statement of the aesthetic that would bring him recognition in *Into the Stone* and *Drowning with Others,* and that he would build on in subsequent books.

"To Be Edward Thomas" appeared in a special 1957 issue of the *Beloit Poetry Journal* dedicated to Robert Frost, in which the magazine's editors "invited poets of many schools and types to send . . . a specifically written poem, one inspired in some way (it need not be directly) by Frost, the man, his poetry or his philosophy."[14] The

12. "A Retrospect," 4, 12.

13. Dickey's exhortations to the literary community in the essay "The Suspect in Poetry or Everyman as Detective" (1960) also echo Pound. Dickey assumes a bold, straightforward tone, presenting himself as an angry, disgusted writer, responding to a crisis in contemporary poetry, who desires to make poetry relevant by ridding it of ornamentation. He asserts that poetry has become an "effrontery" of the reader's sense of truth and reality. Rejecting the "remarkable amount of utter humbug, absolutely and uselessly far-fetched and complex manipulation of language" that he perceives on the contemporary scene, Dickey stresses that a writer must maintain a "fundamental kind of unliterary innocence" to evoke real emotions, and that art only "justifies itself" when the reader is able to forget that his emotions are being "deliberately evoked" (9).

14. Though Dickey had become personally acquainted with Frost at the University of Florida, his subsequent remarks about Frost indicate that he was less than enamored of the older poet. Describing his impression of Frost while both were at the University of Florida, Dickey remarked that he had never seen "a more sententious, holding-forth old bore who expected every hero-worshipping adenoidal little twerp of a student-poet to hang on his every word," and that "if it were ever thought that anything I wrote was influenced by Robert Frost, I would take that particular work of mine, shred it, and flush it down the toilet" ("James Dickey," interview in *Writers at Work,* 219). In fact, though "To Be Edward Thomas" is supposed to be a tribute to Frost, Frost is little more than a prop who provides a

poem begins with a personal recollection of Frost and the narrator—
Dickey's own projection of himself—taking a walk at sunset on a
beach in northern Florida. From its beginning the poem emphasizes
Dickey's subjective and shifting perception of phenomena as light
plays off various objects: the "generalized swaying of moss" be-
comes "faceless beards with the breath of water / Stirring," and
shifts into "a tree of yarn, the wild-wire gentle / Glowing." Through
the light of sunset, Dickey sees in Frost's visage

> all loved old men
> Composed, eroded, in the world's despairing search
> For the time-born, original, singing and featureless face
> That moved upon the making of its waters,
>
> And thought, how vulnerable they are, the old,
> Whose body in every motion is
> Extending back through time.

Dickey's emphasis on perception and transformation indicates
his movement toward subjective narration. As he states in the poem,
his imagination is "assembling" and discovering unity between past
and present in an effort to freeze time in the form of an image.
Unlike Eliot's or Tate's use of the image, which stressed fragmenta-
tion and disjunction, Dickey's use of the image, like Pound's, be-
comes the transcendental center of experience—a means to capture
and freeze time, and invigorate the moment with significance.
    Looking out over the water and the wind-blown saw grass, Dickey's
speaker realizes

> that a part of light would not
> Be there, as it was, without three words:
> "The team's head-brass."

Though the relationship between the "three words" and the "light"
is not exactly clear, Dickey discovers that without the image created
by these words Frost mutters from Edward Thomas's poem "The
Team's Head-Brass," his ability to experience the play of light on the
waves would not be significant. The image allows him to break

---

line, not even from his own poetry, that sparks Dickey's mind.

loose from the grips of mundane sight and discover imaginative vision, resulting in a physical response: this and subsequent events hit him "like a body blow from the / soul." Through the image the poet can "draw off Time" and allow ordinary things to "blaze / with reverence":

> Bark, wind in the interlaced boughs: these beyond
>   Thought, at last,
> What they must surely be: leaves, limbs, beasts, in
>   Their holy reasons:
> Determined by him, but given by the world.

The image lets the poet go "beyond thought," determine the world, and endow it with meaning. Like Pound's stress on the image's potential for discovering "truth," Dickey uses the image as a powerful ordering force that through the special powers of the poet becomes the essential aspect of all human life. Dickey sees the poet as a "maker" of new realities: "Poetry draws on the external world, the God-made world, and the poet makes of it what he will and can. . . . What I say about it is not anything God said. Its what I say."[15]

The narrative-image poems also reflect Pound's emphasis on presentational immediacy, beginning in medias res, plunging the reader directly into the action. However, where Pound's image seizes an "intellectual and emotional complex in an instant of time," Dickey's narrative image captures a psychological and physical effect by describing a brief experience during which the poem's first-person narrator experiences an epiphany resulting in a more unified and aware self. This difference can be traced to what each man views as poetry's function. Unlike Pound's goal of interpretive political and cultural insight, Dickey's concern is with restoring, in Ralph Waldo Emerson's phrase, "an original relationship to the universe."

The succinct, intense narrative-image poems of Dickey's first two books are relatively short, usually less than fifty lines. While containing elements of plot, the poems do not so much unfold in time as concentrate on specific psychological experiences. Through the brief situation presented, Dickey strives to make a visceral imprint

15. Interviews with author, August 8–15, 1989.

on the reader that becomes a lasting part of that person's conscious-
ness. The memory of these narrative images then changes and in-
tensifies the manner in which a person experiences the world, help-
ing create what Pound describes as "that sense of liberation . . . that
sense of freedom from time and space limits . . . that sense of
sudden growth."16

Dickey's "The String," first published in *Poetry* (1959) and later
collected in *Into the Stone,* typifies Dickey's use of narrative in his
first two books. The poem begins with the assertion that the narra-
tor "cannot bring his brother to himself," and it ends with the narra-
tor physically feeling his dead brother's presence in his body. The
emphasis is not so much on what happens physically, as in tradi-
tional narratives, but on the psychological experience the narrator
undergoes, culminating in the poem's final stanza, in which he
realizes that contrary to his statement in the first stanza, his brother
has "completed the maze" of his "fingers":

> Except when he enters my son,
> The same age as he at his death,
> I cannot bring my brother to myself.
> I do not have his memory in my life,
> Yet he is in my mind and on my hands.
> I weave the trivial string upon a light
> *Dead before I was born.*
>
> Mark how the brother must live,
> Who comes through the words of my mother.
> I have been told he lay
> In his death-bed singing with fever,
> Performing with string on his fingers
> Incredible feats of construction
> *There before he was born.*
>
> His Jacob's Coffin now
> Floats deeply between my fingers.
> The strings with my thin bones shake.
> My eyes go from me, and down
> Through my bound, spread hands
> To the dead, from the kin of the dead,
> *Dead before I was born.* (IS, 222)

16. "A Retrospect," 3.

Here, in the first three of the poem's seven stanzas, the narrator manipulates the "trivial string" with his fingers, sparking memories of his dead brother, causing him to begin to enter his brother's life. While there is an emphasis on story and on unfolding of event, as is typical of narrative (we are told about the brother's death and how the narrator was "Out of grief . . . / Conceived, and brought to life / To replace the incredible child"), time and physical action are deemphasized, indeed almost frozen, in favor of the psychological action and insight that occurs at the instant he gazes at the string.

Whether Dickey's narrator is gazing into a string strewn across his fingers and experiencing his dead brother's presence in his body, opening his eyes to the first light of morning and re-creating the world ("Sleeping Out at Easter"), shading his eyes from the sun and remembering a friend executed in the war ("The Performance"), sitting with a dog asleep on his legs and entering that animal's life ("A Dog Sleeping on My Feet"), or hunting as the fog engulfs his body ("Fog Envelops the Animals"), most of the poems of Dickey's first two books arrest a situation into a totalizing image. Dickey's early uncollected poetry and his relationship to Pound are essential to understanding the emergence of that dynamic arrest.

Critics too often focus on the thematic content of Dickey's work and call him a "romantic" or "neoromantic" without comprehending either his debt to Pound's idea of the image or his struggle with New Critical forms. Dickey's aesthetic did not so much develop in opposition to the status and pressure of modernism or New Criticism but *out* of them. Indeed, though the type of encompassing narrative image Dickey captured in his first two books would be impossible to maintain in the longer, more intricately plotted poems of his later work, the image and its ability to allow one to see the world in a fresh manner continues to be the strength and foundation of Dickey's poetry. If looking into the "uncollected Dickey" reveals a literary development less spectacular than the current Dickey "legend" supplies, it also shows us a writer who worked through the heritage of "MODERN POETRY," making the originality he eventually established all the more solidly grounded and impressive.

2

Emerson in Vietnam
Dickey, Bly, and the New Left

James Dickey's career provides an especially clear example of the way history alters and informs the reception of a poet's work. Throughout his literary career, which began in the early fifties, Dickey has expressed the belief that volatile and violent qualities are an inherent and sometimes desirable part of the human condition, while the loss of aggressive, instinctual urges is a form of castration that cuts off access to the full realm of experience. However, in the late sixties Dickey's penchant for stating his views in extreme terms led many critics to accuse him of possessing a brutal sensibility that lacked social consciousness. Attacks on Dickey started in 1967, when Robert Bly called him "sick" and "sadistic" for his treatment of war in *Buckdancer's Choice*. Since then critics have often complained that Dickey's writings lack a moral arbiter. Dickey's use of violence in his writing has been widely viewed as symptomatic of this failure.

Without question, violence and aggression are integral parts of

Dickey's vision, which finds its origins in the Emersonian tradition. Dickey sees history from a philosophically mystical vantage point that identifies violence and disorder as part of a larger scheme based on the primacy of the individual, a view for which the New Left literary establishment condemned him after the escalation of the Vietnam War. Examining these controversial elements of Dickey's poetry by situating them, and the adverse critical reaction to his work, within the historical backdrop of American culture and literature shows how the Vietnam War resulted in critics' valuing the didactical over the dialectical and the communal over the individual. Dickey's complex metaphysics collided with the politics of a historical particular, the war, which generated a critical agenda that could not accommodate the philosophical underpinnings to his poetry. The specific poems I have selected to discuss—"Sleeping Out at Easter," "The Vegetable King," "The Summons," "The Performance," "Between Two Prisoners," "Approaching Prayer," and "The Firebombing"—are representative of the volumes in which they appear, and all point to an Emersonian transcendentalism that perpetuates the metaphysics—and their ideological implications—of the major American visionary poets.

Dickey's conception of the poet's function and effect on the reader distinctly parallels Emerson's. For Emerson, "the poet turns the world to glass, and shows us all things in their rightful series and procession";[1] for Dickey, "there is an essential connection . . . between the world and you, and it is as a divine intermediary between you and the world that poetry functions, bringing with it . . . an enormous increase in perception, an increased ability to understand and interpret the order of one's experience" ("EM," 164). For both men, the visionary act is integrative, allowing one to unify and transfigure experience, or, as Dickey matter-of-factly puts it, "evoke a world that is realer than real" (SP, 76). Like Emerson, Dickey wants his readers to draw upon long-dormant psychic energies in order to discover a direct, active relationship to the world. Similar to Dickey's "energized man," the portrait of "Man-thinking" Emerson presents in "The American Scholar" describes not

---

1. "The Poet," in *Selections from Ralph Waldo Emerson*, ed. Stephen E. Whicher, 230.

just a mind at work but an entire being actively using all of his or her faculties.[2]

In his first two books, *Into the Stone* and *Drowning with Others*, Dickey presents poems that make up a primer for an aesthetics of renewal based on what Emerson called "symbolic perception," an ability to re-see the world again. The majority of these poems are relatively short, typically describing a brief experience during which the poem's first-person narrator undergoes a change that results in a more unified and aware self. In essence these poems are short dramatic parables that show the reader the process of becoming "energized"— Dickey's term for the type of transcendence he desires to induce in his readers. Ideally, participation in what Dickey calls "creative lies" awakens in the reader the potential to realize a similar change.

These aspects of Dickey's poetry are clearly present in "Sleeping Out at Easter" and "The Vegetable King," two poems that show how he perceived the connection between the world and the individual psyche in his early books. "Sleeping Out at Easter" begins in medias res, plunging the reader into the action and providing a sense of spontaneity. The narrator's description of his "resurrection" on Easter morning resonates with Christian and pagan overtones, making the seemingly mundane dramatic situation—a man waking at daybreak after sleeping out in his backyard—assume a mythic, mystic dimension:

> Birds speak, their voices beyond them.
> A light has told them their song.
> My animal eyes become human
> As the Word rises out of the darkness
> Where my right hand, buried beneath me,
> Hoveringly tingles, with grasping

2. Hyatt H. Waggoner, in *American Poetry from the Puritans to the Present*, traces Emerson's importance to subsequent American poets. Waggoner includes brief remarks on the similarities between Emerson's and Dickey's conceptions of the poet. Waggoner's observations in his introduction are of particular interest.

Dickey has long professed the desire to "energize" his readers by getting them to remain receptive to the full spectrum of psychic and physical life. He describes the energized individual as one who "functions with not, say, fifteen percent of his faculties, as advertisers and psychologists say the average man does, but, ideally, with a hundred percent, a veritable walking A-bomb among the animated or half animated spectres of the modern world" ("EM," 165).

> The source of all song at the root.
> *Birds sing, their voices beyond them.*

The steady, flowing, melodic quality of the anapest enhances the feeling that the experience happens without encumbrance. In each of the first five stanzas, the last line repeats or closely echoes the first and is italicized, serving as a refrain and producing the hypnotic quality of an incantation. The sixth and final stanza consists entirely of the italicized refrains. This results in a sense of continuity and unity, as the poem's lines echo themselves as effortlessly as the narrator completely accepts the dawn and his newfound self. Dickey captures an organic unity of theme and technique that arrests and annihilates time through the image of first light, creating a new world around the narrator as he grasps the "root," the "source," of all life and of his most elemental self; it is a moment of pure religious transcendence, involving a sense of immortality achieved through communion with the permanent essence of nature. Here the narrator, and in a larger sense Dickey, who after more than a decade of struggle had become his own poet with his own message to impart, discovers the "Word," Logos.

The poem is more than an account of its narrator, however, for Dickey clearly intends it to initiate change in the reader as well. He directly addresses the reader through the use of second person in the fourth and sixth stanzas (the other four stanzas are presented in first person). These stanzas are completely italicized, indicating a transcendent voice that reverberates through all things. Similarly, the "light" that accompanies the new day spreads everywhere, touching everything simultaneously, symbolizing the renewal and coming together of all things. In the first stanza the man waking declares, "My sight is the same as the sun's," and in the fifth he describes his child, who,

> mouth open, still sleeping,
> Hears the song in the egg of a bird.
> The sun shall have told him that song.

The transformation becomes complete in the poem's last three lines, which also include the reader:

> *The sun shall have told you this song,*
> *For this is the grave of the king;*
> *For the king's grave turns you to light.*

Aside from these two stanzas, Dickey primarily uses first person in "Sleeping Out at Easter," as in most of the narrative-image poems. When the narrator experiences transcendence he enters into a state of unity with nature ("My sight is the same as the sun's"), with the consciousness of the child, and with the reader. The narrator achieves this state without struggle; the tightly controlled, steady—almost monotonous—metrics reflect the ease, godlike power, and control over experience that so distinctly mark Dickey's first two books and, to a lesser extent, his third book, *Helmets.* In these books Dickey never mentions or alludes to the type of Prufrockian metaphysical doubt that Eliot made fashionable. Instead, he uses creative lies to assert his narrators' abilities to rise above generally accepted human limitations.

A companion piece to "Sleeping Out at Easter," "The Vegetable King," illustrates Dickey's emphasis on subjective perception and his tendency to situate violent features within a dialectical framework. Dickey uses an identical dramatic situation in both poems, but while he presents the situation dramatically in "Sleeping Out at Easter," with the narrator participating in the experience almost instinctually, in "The Vegetable King" the reader becomes privy to the cognitive process that brings forth the transformation. After sunset the narrator takes a sleeping bag outside his suburban home and lies down to perform a "ritual" he repeats "One night each April." He urges himself on,

> Remembering, remembering to feel
>
> The still earth turn my house around the sun
> Where all is dark, unhoped-for, and undone.

He then falls into

> a colored sleep
> coming out
> Of the dark side of the sun.

Light and dark, representing the polarities of experience, emanate from the same source and enable the narrator to

> begin to believe a dream
> I never once have had,
> Of being part of the acclaimed rebirth.

The dream the narrator wills himself to believe becomes the necessary catalyst for the transcendental experience; hence, the locus of change is strictly a matter of individual consciousness. While his resurrection brings a feeling of renewal that he fancies makes possible the growth of flowers, the poem ends with the narrator's return to his suburban household and the looks of his "Mother, son, and wife" that "recall" him.

Dickey uses this pattern of departure—imaginative or physical—from the suburban home, engagement in some significant experience, and return in several of his poems of the sixties ("Sleeping Out at Easter," "A Dog Sleeping on My Feet," "The Firebombing," to name a few) and in *Deliverance*, which he had begun to write in 1962. Dickey's narrators return to suburban existence in an altered state, but suburbia remains unchanged, and they do not attempt to alter that.

Like his conception of the poet's function, Dickey's emphasis on the self is remarkably like Emerson's, which also makes the individual the locus of change. Both men view reality from the vantage point of the self, exploring "the force or truth of the individual soul" and maintaining that "the ruin or the blank that we see when we look at nature, is in our own eye."[3] Such emphasis on intensifying

3. Emerson, "Circles" and *Nature*, in *Selections*, 169 and 55. Spurred on by F. O. Matthiessen's *American Renaissance: Art and Expression in the Age of Emerson and Whitman* (1941), a wealth of now well-known books that claim a central position for Emerson in American literature were published during the 1950s and 1960s. Notable examples include Vivian C. Hopkins's *Spires of Form* (1951), Sherman Paul's *Emerson's Angle of Vision: Man and Nature in American Experience* (1952), Charles Feidelson's *Symbolism in American Literature* (1953), Stephen Whicher's *Freedom and Fate* (1953), R. W. B. Lewis's *The American Adam* (1955), Roy Harvey Pearce's *The Continuity of American Poetry* (1965), Joel Porte's *Emerson and Thoreau* (1966), Richard Poirier's *A World Elsewhere* (1966), Michael Cowan's *City of the West* (1967), and Hyatt Waggoner's *American Poetry from the Puritans to the Present* (originally published 1968). Significantly, Waggoner, who sees Emersonianism as the central influence on Amer-

the individual psyche is prevalent in much American literature of the fifties and the sixties, when a renewed interest in Emerson's work occurred. Indeed, despite the impression often left by critics and Dickey himself concerning the wide gulf between Dickey and his contemporaries, Dickey participates in many of the trends of his time. David Riesman's *The Lonely Crowd* (1950), J. D. Salinger's *The Catcher in the Rye* (1951), Jack Kerouac's *On the Road* (1955), Sloan Wilson's *The Man in the Gray Flannel Suit* (1955), and William H. Whyte's *The Organization Man* (1956) were among the many books that expressed dissatisfaction with the tepid malaise their authors saw characterizing post–World War II American culture. All of these works value individual expression over communal political action. Partly because he discovered his poetic aesthetic and his poetic raison d'être in the fifties, Dickey has continued to see poetry as a means of "energizing" the individual.

Many of Dickey's contemporaries, most notably the poets associated with the deep image school, expressed similar beliefs in the late fifties and early sixties. As Richard Sugg has pointed out, much of Bly's poetry "is squarely within the American romantic tradition of Emerson, Whitman, and Hart Crane."[4] Though the pressure of Vietnam compelled Bly and other deep image poets to apply their poetics of transformed individual consciousness to a more political canvas, the ideas behind the deep image movement, particularly its romantic emphasis on "inwardness" and discovering unknown regions of the psyche, did not initially involve political transformation. In fact, Bly had published and praised Dickey's work in his little magazine the *Sixties* in 1964, and he had lauded *Drowning with Others* in *Choice* in 1962.[5] The qualities in Dickey's work that Bly identified as exceptional, such as creating radically subjective and original images to emphasize individual metamorphosis, are those associated with deep image poetry.

But while other visionary poets in the sixties—Bly, Allen Ginsberg, Galway Kinnell—eventually began presenting themselves as

---

ican poetry, concludes the most recent edition of his book (1984) by predicting that Dickey, along with Denise Levertov, will come to be regarded as the two most important contemporary poets.

4. *Robert Bly*, 142.

5. See Bly's "The Work of James Dickey" and "Prose vs. Poetry."

radicals trying to initiate some fundamental change in society, the transformations of self Dickey continued to advocate in his poetry had nothing to do with concrete changes in the social and political sphere. Though Dickey became deeply involved in antiwar candidate Eugene McCarthy's presidential campaign, he continued to associate much of the nonconformity expressed in the sixties with a fifties-like dissatisfaction with American culture. Indeed, Dickey's views on the New Left counterculture typify his tendency to concentrate on paradoxes. Dickey believed that the antiwar counterculture's formation was largely motivated by individuals' search for meaning, even though it involved mass political protest. On *Firing Line* Dickey expressed that there was no "proof . . . humanly capable of being given" that would justify the "sacrifice" of "50,000 American lives and untold billions of dollars" in Vietnam, and that "one must pay attention" to "the public opposition to the war," but he also insisted that Vietnam served as a source of identity for the young: "Vietnam in a sense identifies them. They have an identity which they were afraid of being raped of by middle-class America and the situation in which most of them grew up. The war is something that's important to them because it gives them an identity both as a group and as individuals, just like long hair" (*NH*, 149–50).

In 1971 Dickey professed that "all the revolutions and revolutionary activities of the past ten or fifteen years" were "protests of the increasing trivialization of life" (*S*, 72). In 1972 Dickey even evoked the specter of Wilson's *Man in the Gray Flannel Suit*: "I like the hippies. . . . I think those outlandish costumes they wear are very colorful and nice. . . . They are dead set against this business of being shoved into the gray flannel suit and the gray flannel image. They want to be themselves, even if they don't know who themselves are. They're looking, and I can't help thinking that's a good thing" (*NH*, 420).

Dickey's allusion to Wilson's book, his claims that the tumultuous upheavals of the sixties were reactions to the "increasing trivialization of life," and his view that young people "were afraid of being raped" of their identities by "middle-class America," all describe sixties nonconformity in terms characteristic of reactions to revolts against Eisenhower republicanism in the fifties. Rather than being solely provoked by the policies of the Vietnam era, Dickey thinks the sixties antiwar and counterculture movements also emerged from a pervasive sense that social existence had become meaningless. Although the political circumstances surrounding Vietnam provided a channel or focus for widespread discontent, Dickey believes that in contemporary America nonconformity and rebellion are largely motivated by a quest for identity.

Accordingly, Dickey continues to insist upon the essential privacy of the individual. He thinks that poetry enriches through the intensity experienced by a reader alone with the poems. Dickey views himself as a tribal singer and seeks to move the masses, but not as "the people." Consequently, his poetic parables are designed to affect the individual self in a private manner. Where Ginsberg, Bly, Kinnell, and others felt fundamental political change was essential in the sixties and expressed it through the subject matter of their poetry, Dickey sought to energize individuals by providing images that allowed them to see their world in some unique way.

Dickey's attitude toward the relationship between the individual and society is also remarkably like Emerson's. Emerson professes that people's vision has become passive because they respond to the world only according to custom, and, in Dickey's words, "with drift, habit, and the general sense of the purposelessness of life sets in a genuine malaise" ("IG," 163). Though living in an organized society perpetuates the customs and habits that contribute to this condition, for both writers the essential variable that must change is the way in which people perceive themselves and the world. Fundamental concrete changes in the social structure are not essential parts of their prescriptions. A passage from "The American Scholar" reveals Emerson's focus:

> The state of society is one in which the members have suffered amputation from the trunk, and strut about so many walking monsters,—a good finger, a neck, a stomach, an elbow, but never a man. Man is thus metamorphosed into a thing, into many things. The planter, who is Man sent out into the field to gather food, is seldom cheered by any idea of the true integrity of his ministry. He sees his bushel and his cart, and nothing beyond, and sinks into the farmer, instead of Man on the farm.[6]

6. "The American Scholar," in Selections, 64–65.

Though Emerson blames "the state of society" and the increased division of labor for causing the dilemma, he does not argue for a change in the system but insists that people's attitude toward their work must change. In urging the farmer to become "Man on the farm," Emerson asks him to realize the "true integrity" of his work, improving his life by enlarging his consciousness but without fundamental alterations of the social order. Likewise, Dickey, in his effort to "energize" people, does not want to alter suburbia materially but change suburban man into Man in suburbia. He wants to deliver people from "a sense of purposelessness, of drift, of just getting along from day to day, of using only those faculties which we must use in order to earn a living, or in order to experience a few of those well-known physical pleasures so dear to the American heart" ("IG," 163). For both men, the oppressor is not a particular system of government or a particular social order but the inherent monotony in *any* civilization. The remedy for such a condition resides in realizing the wonder one can discover when performing acts like plowing a field or sleeping out in the backyard.

Consistent with this belief, Dickey's concerns involve examining the relationship between romantic individualism and power. In Dickey's work we discover a strange brew of existentialist and romantic philosophy, which helps account for the virulent critical reactions he drew in the late sixties. In 1989 Dickey told me that when he met Yvor Winters, Winters said that Dickey was "essentially an American decadent romantic poet following Emerson." Dickey called Winters a "fascistic type" and praised Emerson's directives privileging intuition over reason, declaring, "Honest reaction to experience, intuitive reaction—nothing is of greater consequence than that." Dickey also stated that he liked Emerson's idea that one could "have a direct line to God," but that he could not believe the concept's literal truth. Dickey found no moral guide in Nature, unlike Emerson, who posited the existence of an "Oversoul" with which the individual conspires to serve as a moral center. The "real god is what causes everything to exist, like the laws of motion," but the idea of a moral force governing the universe—especially in respect to human notions of morality—Dickey called "absurd."[7]

7. "Interview with James Dickey," 121–22.

Winters's essay "The Significance of 'The Bridge' by Hart Crane" elaborates his comment to Dickey and directly bears on many critics' reactions to Dickey in the late sixties. Winters blamed Emersonian ideas (via Walt Whitman) for leading to Hart Crane's death. He believed Crane was essentially a religious poet, but one whose religion entailed an absolute faith in impulse and intuition, rather than in any rational conception of God or morality. Winters felt that the "social restraints, the products of generations of discipline, which operated to minimize the influence of Romantic philosophy in the personal lives of Emerson and Whitman, were at most only slightly operative in Crane's career," and that without such restraints "madness" and "suicide" were the "inevitable" consequences of putting the "doctrine of Emerson and Whitman . . . into practice." When Winters told Crane that he found Emerson's doctrines unbelievable, Crane declared, "Well, if we can't believe it, we'll have to kid ourselves into believing it."[8] As Winters pointed out, Crane was expressing much this same sentiment in "The Dance" section of "The Bridge," when the narrator pleads with the Indian medicine man to "Lie to us! Dance us back the tribal morn!"

When Winters called Dickey an "American decadent romantic poet following Emerson," he no doubt had these very ideas in mind. Dickey's emphasis on "creative lies" are his way of dancing the reader back to the "tribal morn." In "The Suspect in Poetry or Everyman as Detective," published in the same year as *Into the Stone,* Dickey indicated his acute concern with a poem's religious effect on the reader: "What matters is that there be some real response to poems: that for certain people there be certain poems that speak as directly to them as they believe God would" (*SP,* 10). But Dickey, living in an age even farther removed from the "social restraints, the products of generations of discipline" than Crane, presents a religion of naturalistic forces and of *willed* sensation.

For Emerson, transcendence means passing beyond generally accepted human limitations to discover a connection with an "Oversoul" that exists. This supernatural entity guides the individual, rewarding good behavior while punishing wrongdoing. For instance, in "Compensation" Emerson sets out to refute doctrines that

8. *In Defense of Reason: Primitivism and Decadence,* 589–90, 579.

claim that "judgment is not executed in this world." Dickey's meta-physics are immanent rather than transient, however. Morality becomes a subjective construct devoid of a supernatural touchstone. Dickey believes that "man no longer has to depend on any super-naturalisms, nor *can* he rely on them. . . . Man is essentially what he has made of himself" (*NH*, 91). Dickey desires to reconnect with intuitive, basic forces, but he finds no god or "Oversoul" to help mediate the process. Dickey's individual must engage in an action—artistic, psychological, or physical—that *makes* a new reality spring forth ("Man is free to act, but man must act to be free"). Dickey's creative lies address the nausea he senses in a society where people "sit down and have a martini and look at television. . . . The suburban life comes out to be a kind of condition of inconsequentiality; you feel that you live with your head packed in cotton. There is no reality" (*NH*, 94). But while Dickey believes in the importance of "intuitive reaction" in combating existential angst, he also believes that such a response has a destructive side, in contrast to Bly and Ginsberg, who both see "impulse" as a salutary purgative from an oppressive commercialized society.

Dickey's Emersonianism is not innocent but propelled into a value-free world where no objective moral standards exist. Dickey claims that the combination of "the need for some kind of adrenalin in your body," which gives "the sense of living on the edge" and "significance to things," and the security and comfort that America's relatively affluent life affords can be "an intolerable match up" because it creates "the Lee Harvey Oswalds of the world," who "would rather be murderers than be the nothings that they are" (*NH*, 95–96). Out of Dickey's belief in this condition arise characters like "The Fiend," a clerk who escapes his inconsequential existence by engaging in voyeurism and murder. In such poems Dickey gives us the world Winters feared. While Dickey sees Winters's antidote to Romantic philosophy—rationalism and order—as creating the need for actions based on impulse, he also regards such actions as potentially diabolical.

On the surface, much in the New Left—irrational mysticism and the instinctual—should have been agreeable to Dickey, but his belief in people's destructive potential causes him to depict reactions against mainstream culture as a double-edged sword that can pare

conformity but also wound. Dickey's beliefs are incongruent with
Winters's ordered world of high culture and Bly's New Left coun-
terculture. In *Deliverance*, for example, the suburbanites engage in
an experience designed to help them break away from routine exis-
tence, but the cost includes death and rape at the hands of truly
primitive men who follow their impulses without vacillation.

This volatile combination of contradictory messages, in which the
"cure" is potentially a life-affirming *and/or* a destructive, atavistic
reawakening, unsettled the New Left literati, who had a tendency
to embrace utopian solutions. In sharp contrast to the New Left's
idealism, Dickey presents a world where violence, love, pain, plea-
sure, death, and life are all vividly present and, at times, even
indistinguishable. As a result, situations or emotional states in Dickey's
poems are seldom characterized by one overpowering sensation
but present a mixture of contradictory forces. In "The Vegetable
King" the narrator brings home "pardon," "dread," and "crime"
and makes himself believe he is "part of the acclaimed rebirth,"
identifying with Christ's resurrection yet invoking "the gods and
animals of Heaven," who, like the narrator, are "mismade inspir-
ingly." These lines point to an important component of Dickey's
metaphysics: the god summoned in "The Vegetable King" is not the
nonviolent, idealistic god of the New Testament, but the sort found
in Greek mythology. To be "mismade" is inspiring because it allows
one to participate in the entire gamut of experience. Thus in order
to bring new life to himself and his surroundings, the narrator must
believe himself "hacked apart in the growing cold" before being
reassembled by "the whole of mindless nature." To embrace all
aspects of experience as they exist, and to see and celebrate their
unity, becomes the vehicle of transcendence.

Dickey's "The Summons," from *Drowning with Others*, embodies
such an attitude: the poem shows love and killing as part of the
same transcendent experience. "The Summons" begins with the
narrator cupping a blade of grass in his hand and issuing a call "no
hunter has taught" him; instead, "it comes out of childhood and
playgrounds." As the narrator continues to make the call

> some being stumbles,
> And answers me slowly and greatly

With a tongue as rasping as sawgrass.
I lower my hands, and I listen
To the beast that shall die of its love.
I sound my green trumpet again,
And the whole wood sings in my palms.

The call, which results in killing and death by bringing the hunter and the animal together, operates as a source of unity: it mixes with the wind, making "it live"; the lake "contains the sound" that "encircles the forest"; the "whole wood sings in" his "palm." Death and killing are essential components of this unity. The playground call becomes a complex song of nature, yoking the contraries of death, violence, innocence, and love:

The vast trees are tuned to my bowstring

And the deep-rooted voice I have summoned.
I have carried it here from a playground
Where I rolled in the grass with my brothers.
Nothing moves, but something intends to.
The water that puffed like a wing
Is one flattened blaze through the branches.
Something falls from the bank, and is swimming.
My voice turns around me like foliage,

And I pluck my longbow off the limb
Where it shines with a musical light,
And crouch within death, awaiting
The beast in the water, in love
With the palest and gentlest of children,
Whom the years have turned deadly with knowledge:
Who summons him forth, and now
Pulls wide the great, thoughtful arrow.

The weapon, the hunter, the call, and the killing are not viewed as outside elements infringing on nature but as an integral part of the process of life. Dickey describes the weapon in terms that suggest harmony with its surroundings: the bow is "tuned" to the trees and gives off "a musical light"; the arrow is "great" and "thoughtful"— thoughtful because Dickey portrays the killing not as an arbitrary act but part of a purposeful design. The poem celebrates that design, and the animal is "summoned" to fulfill his role. Likewise, the hunter, who is described in terms likening him to Apollo, can "crouch within death" because he, "whom the years have turned deadly with knowledge," realizes his role.

Dickey's war poems also reflect his tendency to stress the individual and the paradoxical, frequently emphasizing the unique insight that extreme, and often violent, situations can yield, rather than explicitly protesting against the existence of such situations. "The Performance" (1960), one of Dickey's first compelling poems, illustrates his Emersonian emphasis. Dickey describes "The Performance," a tribute to a fellow pilot who was his "best friend in the squadron," as a poem in which "almost every word . . . is literally true, except that the interpretation of the facts is my own" (SI, 92). During World War II Dickey's friend, Donald Armstrong, was forced to crash-land a P-61 while on a strafing mission on Panay. Japanese soldiers captured Armstrong and beheaded him the next day.

Dickey stresses the force of the individual psyche, as the poem's narrator enters into a reverie in which he imagines Armstrong's death. The narrator remembers that the last time he saw Armstrong, his friend was on a Philippine island practicing handstands. Though Armstrong staggers

> unbalanced, with his big feet looming and waving
> In the great, untrustworthy air
> He flew in each night

he continues to practice in order to "perfect his role." The next day Armstrong is taken prisoner and executed. The narrator imagines Armstrong's performance before his captors:

> Doing all his lean tricks to amaze them—
> The back somersault, the kip-up—
> And at last, the stand on his hands,
> Perfect, with his feet together,
> His head down, evenly breathing,
> As the sun poured up from the sea
>
> And the headsman broke down
> In a blaze of tears, in that light
> Of the thin, long human frame
> Upside down in its own strange joy,
> And, if some other one had not told him,
> Would have cut off the feet

> Instead of the head,
> And if Armstrong had not presently risen
> In kingly, round-shouldered attendance,
> And then knelt down in himself
> Beside his hacked, glittering grave, having done
> All things in this life that he could.

Here the creative lie, which portrays Armstrong doing gymnastic tricks, adds a sense of mystery to the situation, emphasizing the moment's revelatory quality. Armstrong perfects the handstand and dies in imagined glory—implied by the image in the last stanza of him being knighted as he is beheaded—"having done / All things in this life that he could." However, Armstrong's transformation only exists for the narrator, who is remembering the last time he saw his friend, but who was not present at the execution. The narrator creates a unity to his memory of Armstrong's life, but Armstrong remains unaffected. No anger or moral judgment concerning the injustice of the situation is expressed, nor is Armstrong's death lamented; such issues are never addressed. Instead, war and death are accepted as givens, and the power of subjective perception is foregrounded.

Typical of Dickey's war poems, "Between Two Prisoners" also emphasizes the subjective reality of the individual and the paradoxical nature of the visionary moment. In the poem Dickey shows that the captor is in many ways just as trapped as the captive. To create the poem, Dickey drew on information he had obtained from Filipino guerrillas, who told him Armstrong and another prisoner, Jim Lalley, were held in an abandoned schoolhouse and tied with wire to children's desks until they were executed the next morning. Though the first half of the poem concentrates on the prisoners' situation and reactions, midway through the poem the primary concern becomes the guards' actions and reactions. The poem opens with the narrator's declaration,

> I would not wish to sit
> In my shape bound together with wire,
> Wedged into a child's sprained desk
> In the schoolhouse under the palm tree.
> Only those who did could have done it.

The last line of this stanza provides a key to the poem. The line could be translated, "Only those who have been cast in such a role know what such a performance entails." As the poem develops, the extreme situation serves as a catalyst for revelation. This becomes equally true for the role the guard must perform.

The dramatic situation in which Dickey places the guard reflects his emphasis on paradox. The guard finds himself, as the poem's title indicates, caught "Between Two Prisoners." The prisoners develop a special communication between them, as "a belief in words grew upon them / That the unbound, who walk, cannot know." The guard, who has fallen asleep, also becomes privy to this special language. He can "hear, in a foreign tongue, / All things that cannot be said." As the prisoners talk to each other they gain vision. Out of the "deep signs carved in the desk tops" by the children who once inhabited the schoolhouse and the "signs on the empty blackboard," a burst of colors appears, evolving into the shape of an angel, "casting green, ragged bolts / Each having the shape of a palm leaf." The palm leaf suggests peace and reconciliation, and the figure of the sleeping guard, emitting "red," bloodlike tears, also becomes luminous, suggesting his spiritual salvation. The guard's redemption is also implied when the two prisoners' voices enter his consciousness as he sleeps. In the morning, when the guard awakes, he discovers "he had talked to himself/ All night, in two voices, of Heaven."

Later, the guard suffers a fate similar to the prisoners':

> I watched the small guard be hanged
> A year later, to the day,
> In a closed horse stall in Manila.
> No one knows what language he spoke
> As his face changed into all colors,
>
> And gave off his red, promised tears,
> Or if he learned blindly to read
> A child's deep, hacked hieroglyphics
> Which can call up an angel from nothing,
> Or what was said for an instant, there,
>
> In the tied, scribbled dark, between him
> And a figure drawn hugely in chalk,
> Speaking words that can never be spoken

> Except in a foreign tongue,
> In the end, at the end of a war.

As in "The Performance," in "Between Two Prisoners" Dickey focuses on individual revelation without issuing an explicit moral pronouncement. His suggestion that the guard experienced a visionary moment similar to that of the prisoners', and that the guard's experience was even a result of his relationship with the prisoners, goes beyond absolving the guard of any blame; it indicates that the prisoners and the guard share a spiritual bond. The common bond of death and war brings the characters to this union. While the narrator asserts that such situations are not desirable ("I would not wish to sit / In my shape bound together with wire"), the knowledge the characters gain is made possible by the torturous events. The drastic circumstances push the soldiers' thoughts toward revelation, and the narrator reports this paradoxical occurrence without moral evaluation.

In *Helmets* Dickey continued to explore the themes of his earlier poetry; nevertheless, *Helmets* represents a transitional volume in the Dickey canon. While there are still many short poems relying on intense narrative images—poems that express control and metaphysical certainty—there also appear longer, more diffuse poems that suggest doubt and a reduced sense of control. While some of the poems in *Into the Stone* and *Drowning with Others* draw upon the everyday, the emphasis is, with one or two exceptions like "A Screened in Porch in the Country," on achieving a "superhuman" transcendent state, and transcendence is always gained. Though there are still plenty of poems of this kind in *Helmets*, in some of the poems—"Cherry Log Road," "The Scarred Girl"—the epiphanies are more modest and more fully human. And other poems— "Springer Mountain" and "Kudzu"—represent a more purely comic vein than his previous work. "Approaching Prayer," one of Dickey's finest poems, indicates the manner in which the visionary moment and the role of violence began to evolve in Dickey's later work.

"Approaching Prayer" begins,

> A moment tries to come in
> Through the windows, when one must go
> Beyond what there is in the room, . . .

Instead of plunging the reader right into a religious experience as in "Sleeping Out at Easter," or into the cognitive process leading directly to that experience as in "The Vegetable King," we witness a struggle:

> And I must get up and start
> To circle through my father's empty house
> Looking for things to put on
> Or to strip myself of
> So that I can fall to my knees
> And produce a word I can't say
> Until all my reason is slain.

To slay "reason" so that the imagination can expand toward spiritual unity is the very purpose of the narrative-image poems and a central demand Dickey makes on his readers. But here, rather than lying (in both senses of the word) in a sleeping bag and remembering to feel exactly what he needs to feel, or lying in "The Mountain Tent" and "hearing the shape of the rain / Take the shape of the tent and believe it," effortlessly becoming attuned to "a profound, unspeakable law," the narrator wanders around uncertain of what he is doing. He must "circle" and go "looking for things" before he can "produce a word" he isn't even sure of.

Like an amateur shaman he begins to dress for a ritual ceremony he has never previously performed:

> Here is the gray sweater
> My father wore in the cold,
> The snapped threads growing all over it
> Like his gray body hair.
> The spurs of his gamecocks glimmer
> Also, in my light, dry hand.
> And here is the head of a boar
> I once helped to kill with two arrows:
>
> Two things of my father's
> Wild, Bible-reading life
> And my own best and stillest moment
> In a hog's head waiting for glory.

The objects the narrator picks up encompass a range of experience and retain contradictory associations. The things he gathers before attempting prayer are all associated with death—the head of a boar he killed, his dead father's sweater, and gamecock spurs. The objects also hold positive value: the hog's head represents the narrator's "best and stillest moment"; the spurs and sweater contain the memory of his father. The spurs and the hog's head are also associated with violence, and the narrator declares that his "best" moment involved violence:

> All these I set up in the attic,
> The boar's head, gaffs, and the sweater
> On a chair, and gaze in the dark
> Up into the boar's painted gullet.
>
> Nothing. Perhaps I should feel more foolish,
> Even, than this.

The narrator's self-consciousness gets in the way of his attempt to subdue reason, free the imagination, and enter prayer. The moment is both humorous and absurd. Dickey had displayed moments of humor in previous poems—like the dark humor of picturing Donald Armstrong doing gymnastic tricks before being beheaded—and he has stated, "I don't think you can get to sublimity without courting the ridiculous" (SI, 65). Though having a character reach transcendence by sleeping in his backyard or gazing into a children's string game does court the ridiculous, here the humor is directed at the very attempt to enter the transcendent state, suggesting that the prospect of attaining such an end might be futile. Gazing at the objects results in "nothing." The narrator gathers the objects together, but just being in their presence is not enough. Dickey's brand of animism requires that the narrator enter into an active, physical relationship with the objects:

> I put on the ravelled nerves
>
> And gray hairs of my tall father
> In the dry grave growing like fleece,
> Strap his bird spurs to my heels
> And kneel down under the skylight.
> I put on the hollow hog's head
> Gazing straight up

> With star points in the glass eyes
> That would blind anything that looked in
>
> And cause it to utter words.

The simile previously used to describe the sweater is now dropped. When the narrator enters into an active relationship with the object, imaginative transformation ensues: the sweater *becomes* his father's "ravelled nerves / And gray hairs." After putting on the objects, the narrator begins to discover another "best and stillest moment" through the dead hog's glass eyes by lining himself up with the stars in the night sky. Once centered, words become symbols of spiritual facts (again suggestive of Emerson's conception of language): "words" mediate vision, functioning, as Dickey remarks about poetry, as "divine intermediary" between people and the world ("EM," 164). Poetry ("words"), vision, the imaginative, and the physical are inseparable components of the experience:

> The night sky fills with a light
>
> Of hunting: with leaves
> And sweat and the panting of dogs
>
> Where one tries hard to draw breath,
> A single breath, and hold it.
> I draw the breath of life
> For the dead hog:
> I catch it from the still air,
> Hold it in the boar's rigid mouth,
> And see
>
>> *A young aging man with a bow*
>> *And a green arrow pulled to his cheek*
>> *Standing deep in a mountain creek bed,*
>> *Stiller than trees or stones,*
>> *Waiting and staring.*

The vision explodes before him: "hunting" and being hunted become symbolic of the visionary moment. Similar to "The Summons," where love and killing are linked through hunting, resulting in a transcendent moment, "Approaching Prayer" emphasizes the paradoxical nature of the event: the narrator must experience the contrary roles. Hunting involves physical action requiring discipline and spontaneity; it also contains a deeply imaginative quality. In playing out their particular parts, the predator and the prey each imaginatively enters the other's consciousness. The man must be able to think like the beast, and the beast must try to anticipate the man. When the narrator draws "the breath of life / For the dead hog" he begins to experience the role of the prey. He is able to see himself through the eyes of the other, and a greater range of knowledge begins to open up before him:

> Beasts, angels,
> I am nearly that motionless now
>
> > *There is a frantic leaping at my sides*
> > *Of dogs coming out of the water*
>
> The moon and the stars do not move
>
> > *I bare my teeth, and my mouth*
> > *Opens, a foot long, popping with tushes*
>
> A word goes through my closed lips
>
> > *I gore a dog, he falls, falls back*
> > *Still snapping, turns away and dies*
> > *While swimming. I feel each hair on my back*
> > *Stand up through the eye of a needle*
>
> Where the hair was
> On my head stands up
> As if it were there.

He sees himself from the perspective of the hog, "stiller than trees or stones." His remark, "I am nearly that motionless now," applies both to the moment he participated in the hunt and the instant he experiences in the attic. Here Dickey tries to capture the type of moment he had described when quoting Katherine Anne Porter in a lecture to the Library of Congress: a moment where one lives "'deeply and consistently in that undistracted center of being where the will does not intrude, and the sense of time passing is lost, or has no power over the imagination'" (SC, 14). Stillness, the image of himself as hunter, prey, and man praying that he freezes in his mind, sheers away time. As the narrator imagines himself goring the dog and experiences the hair on his/the hog's back stand, he feels the hair that was on his head as a young man also stand.

Through this thoroughly original moment, the past and the present, and the perspective of predator and prey, merge:

> *The man is still; he is stiller: still*

Yes.

> *Something comes out of him*
> *Like a shaft of sunlight or starlight.*
> *I go forward toward him*

(Beasts, angels)

> *With light standing through me,*
> *Covered with dogs, but the water*
> *Tilts to the sound of the bowstring*

The planets attune all their orbits

> *The sound from his fingers,*
> *Like a plucked word, quickly pierces*
> *Me again, the trees try to dance*
> *Clumsily out of the wood.*

"Yes" signals the release of the arrow; it also signals the narrator's acceptance of life and death. As he experiences killing and being killed at the same instant, the universe comes into balance. This balance consists of stillness and motion—a universe where "the moon and the stars do not move," and where "frantic," violent action takes place. The arrow, characterized as a shaft of light—symbolic of unity and revelation—connects the hunter and the hog. Pain and ecstasy, death and life flood through him as the vision spins to its frenzied conclusion:

I have said something else

> *And underneath, underwater,*
> *In the creek bed are dancing*
> *The sleepy pebbles*

The universe is creaking like boards
Thumping with heartbeats
And bonebeats

> *And every image of death*
> *In my head turns red with blood.*
> *The man of blood does not move*

My father is pale on my body

The dogs of blood
Hang to my ears,
The shadowy bones of the limbs
The sun lays on the water
Mass darkly together

Moonlight, moonlight

The sun mounts my hackles
And I fall; I roll
In the water;
My tongue spills blood
Bound for the ocean;
It moves away, and I see
The trees strain and part, see him
Look upward.

The narrator's unity of consciousness as hunter, prey, and man in the attic praying is conveyed through a series of associations. The "plucked word" the hog hears triggers the thought, "I have said something else," in the man praying, and the hog's thought of pebbles in the creek sets off the creaking of the universe. The pulsing, beating rhythm of the verse, beginning with the strong *nd* emphasis in the line "And underneath, underwater" and continuing through the next six stanzas, breathes outward through *b, d,* and *t* sounds, moving toward expansiveness and unity. The blood-red image of death in the hog's mind becomes the man of blood and dogs of blood. The narrator feels his dead father upon him, and as the blood from the hog's "tongue spills," it merges with water "bound for the ocean," spreading, in Whitman's words, the "delicious word death / And again death, death, death."

The last thing the narrator/hog sees is himself as hunter, directly connecting to the next stanza:

Inside the hair helmet
I look upward out of the total
Stillness of killing with arrows.
I have seen the hog see me kill him
And I was as still as I hoped.
I am that still now, and now.
My father's sweater

Swarms over me in the dark.
I see nothing, but for a second

Something goes through me
Like an accident, a negligent glance,
Like the explosion of a star
Six billion light years off
Whose light gives out

Just as it goes straight through me.
The boar's blood is sailing through rivers
Bearing the living image
Of my most murderous stillness.
It picks up speed
And my heart pounds.
The chicken-blood rust at my heels
Freshens, as though near a death wound
Or flight. I nearly lift
From the floor, from my father's grave
Crawling over my chest

Looking out into the cosmos the narrator has witnessed the hog see him as hunter. This culminates in a unity of vision that allows him to maintain his "stillest" moment until something he compares to a shaft of light from an exploding star, suggestive of the light that connected hunter and hog, shoots through him, letting him feel his own death. At this point he has participated in the complete gamut of life and death: he has seen his death as a "beast" through the eyes of the hog and as an "angel"; he has felt the light of the cosmos flare through him. When his death becomes a reality for him, he realizes that the full cycle of life contains death and violence for himself as well as for the "other." Prayer here does not result in discovery of a god who holds out the promise of an immortal soul, but in a vision that holds many dimensions of experience. Only through experiencing the "contraries" can real prayer be achieved because only through full knowledge of those contraries can life be fully comprehended.

The fresh blood on the spurs symbolizes how close and real the experience has been for the narrator. Like the gamecock he thinks of, he is caught between "the death wound" and "flight." The power and terror of the experience cause the narrator to strip off the articles and vow to "never come back." As he tries to come to grips with the experience, he hopes that he can now

answer what questions men asked
In Heaven's tongue,
Using images of earth
Almightily:
    PROPHECIES, FIRE IN THE SINFUL TOWERS,
    WASTE AND FRUITION IN THE LAND,
    CORN, LOCUSTS AND ASHES,
    THE LION'S SKULL PULSING WITH HONEY,
    THE BLOOD OF THE FIRST-BORN,
    A GIRL MADE PREGNANT WITH A GLANCE
    LIKE AN EXPLODING STAR
    AND A CHILD BORN OF UTTER LIGHT—

Where I can say only, and truly,
That my stillness was violent enough,
That my brain had blood enough,
That my right hand was steady enough,
That the warmth of my father's wool grave
Imparted love enough
And the keen heels of feathery slaughter
Provided lift enough,
That reason was dead enough
For something important to be:

That, if not heard,
It may have been somehow said.

The narrator, like people before him, can only rely on images of the earth to explain existence. Like the vision he has experienced, the images he catalogs from the Bible are scenes containing violence and death as well as creation and life. The narrator is also "BORN OF UTTER LIGHT"—a visionary flash that causes him to experience death and life. Likewise, the prayer need not be "heard" because in his work Dickey never casts a god who makes and determines moral judgments: growth lies in the narrator's new awareness and knowledge of life's forces.

The greater length and the variety of metrical structure of "Approaching Prayer" demonstrate Dickey's increased poetical confidence and flexibility. In contrast, the tightly structured narrative-image poems insist on transcendence, and their relatively short format makes it essential that the experience immediately burst forth or risk losing the impact on the reader altogether. "Approaching Prayer" also indicates Dickey's willingness to more fully and

profoundly question and explore his metaphysics, a pattern that
has continued throughout his career.

As I have suggested, Dickey's tendency to regard violent forces
not as anomalies but as a part of existence is an attitude characteris-
tic of American visionary poets, who have traditionally experienced
difficulty identifying "evil" in their designs because their purpose
has been to understand and unify. In rapturous moments in his
essays Emerson could make statements to the effect that once hu-
man "vision" was completely restored, "so fast will all disagreeable
appearances, swine, spiders, snakes, pests, mad-houses, prisons,
enemies, vanish,"[9] but his more typical approach is expressed in
poems such as "Brahma" or in these lines from "The Sphinx,"
where he views the dualities of existence as necessary components
to the whole of life:

> Eterne alteration
> Now follows, now flies;
> And under pain, pleasure,—
> Under pleasure, pain lies.

While Dickey's extremes are more extreme than Emerson's, both
men account for violence or pain by assimilating the negative fea-
tures of experience into the general process of life. Dickey's narrator
does not condemn "The Fiend" but simply describes him and his
actions. For Dickey, he exists as an undeniable component of the
modern world. Whitman, Crane, and Roethke all display a similar
way of dealing with the negative. A look at representative poems by
each of these writers—for instance "Song of Myself," "The Bridge,"
"Cuttings (later)"—would bear this out.

Until the sixties, the project of the American visionary poet, un-
like Blake or Shelley, had not been to enact political change through
prophetic utopian visions; instead, the American visionary poet
typically took elements or emotions that seemed disparate and rec-
onciled them to show a connection that already existed but was not
apparent—something that readers never realized or that needed to
be reestablished. Thus the pre-sixties American visionary poet tended
to focus on what was already there rather than what could be, and

9. *Nature*, in *Selections*, 56.

the poetry tended to be more realistic than allegorical: there is no "Urizen" or "Prometheus Unbound" among the works of American visionary poets. For the American visionary poet, the message was, "What we have here is enough if we can view it in the right way."

This factor helps account for the decidedly *realistic* component to this essentially romantic genre. The almost journalistic observation and detail found in places in Whitman's, Crane's, Roethke's, and Dickey's work (e.g., catalogs, arrays) implies that a convincing and exact portrait establishes that what already exists in many ways *is* the vision. The creed of the American visionary poet is best expressed in a sentence from the preface to the 1855 edition of *Leaves of Grass:* "The poetic quality is not marshalled in rhyme or uniformity or abstract addresses to things nor in melancholy complaints or good precepts, but is the life of these and much else and is in the soul."

To some critics, Whitman's statement, like Emerson's and Dickey's decision to focus on the self, might seem a passive acceptance of America's political and social circumstance. Visionary realism could be seen as a means of reinforcing, or even actively theorizing, the status quo. But such an interpretation fails to take into account that such poetry strives to reach a greater understanding of what exists; indeed, this understanding is the vision. For instance, "Between Two Prisoners" reveals that the captors and the captives share a human and spiritual bond, but they are forced into the dilemma because of forces beyond their control. War and violence are situated within a dialectic that generates the visionary insight. This is what Dickey means when he asserts that his poems have "an implicit moral stance."[10] But, as I will show, the Vietnam milieu resulted in much literary criticism privileging the didactic over the dialectical, resulting in criticism where subtleties were lost or misinterpreted.

The rise and fall of Dickey's critical reputation provides an excellent example of how historical events shape critics' responses. During the mid sixties Dickey's reputation underwent a meteoric rise because people read his poems as a critique of sentimentality. Critics

10. "Interview with James Dickey," 122.

praised his ability to deal with a wide range of emotions and expe-
riences. *Into the Stone* and *Drowning with Others* were very well
received, and *Helmets* was nominated for the National Book Award.
The *Nation* claimed that unlike most poets, Dickey provided "the
real tooth and claw"; the *Atlantic* declared that Dickey and Lowell
were the only living "major" American poets; the *New York Times
Book Review* heralded him as one of America's most important
poets; the *Chicago Sun-Times* pronounced him the most important
critic of contemporary poetry. These reviews, and many others,
lauded Dickey's poetry and criticism for its honesty and integrity.[11]

One such honest poem, however, significantly changed the direc-
tion of Dickey's career. In 1965 Dickey published "The Firebomb-
ing," in which a middle-aged American confronts his participation
in "anti-morale" bombing missions of Japanese civilians. "The Fire-
bombing," like "Between Two Prisoners," "The Performance," and
all of Dickey's war poems, is based on actual experiences; it ex-
plores the various dimensions of painful events that did occur in
order to furnish insight into those events. "The Firebombing" draws
on Dickey's experiences as a member of the 418 Night-Fighter air
squadron in World War II. Widely praised, the poem was the central
piece in *Buckdancer's Choice*, which won the National Book Award in
1966; but a year later Robert Bly put together an issue of the *Sixties*
featuring "The Collapse of James Dickey" and condemning "The
Firebombing." At the time Bly was the cochairman of American
Writers Against the Vietnam War, and he was leading antiwar pro-
tests at college campuses nationwide. Perhaps because Dickey was
working for a political candidate and living in Washington while
serving as Consultant in Poetry to the Library of Congress, Bly
claimed Dickey was "a toady to the government." Though Dickey
was working for Eugene McCarthy, and had made suggestions for
several anti–Vietnam War speeches, Bly declared Dickey was in
favor of the war and denounced "The Firebombing" as "sadistic."[12]

11. Michael Goldman, "Inventing the American Heart," 530; Peter Davison, "The
Difficulties of Being Major"; X. J. Kennedy, "Joys, Griefs, and 'All Things Innocent,
Hapless, Forsaken,'" 5; Ralph J. Mills, "Brilliant Essays on Contemporary Poetry," 4.

12. Letters between Dickey and McCarthy and Elizabeth Janeway that demon-
strate Dickey's involvement in McCarthy's presidential campaign are on deposit at
the University of South Carolina library.

To Bly, Dickey's visionary realism was an "easy acceptance of brutality," a quality he identified as "deeply middle-class":

> As a poet and a man, Mr. Dickey's attitudes are indistinguishable from standard middle-class attitudes. One cannot help but feel that his depressing collapse represents some obscure defeat for America also. He began writing about 1950, writing honest criticism and sensitive poetry, and suddenly at the age of forty-three, we have a huge blubbering poet, pulling out southern language in long strings, like taffy, a toady to the government, supporting all movements towards empire, a sort of Georgia cracker Kipling.[13]

Despite his work for McCarthy, which went largely unnoticed, Dickey's reputation never recovered among the antiwar literary community after Bly's attack. As sentiment in the academic and literary community began to turn against the Vietnam War in the mid-to-late sixties, denunciations like Bly's became increasingly widespread.

Bly's attack includes a number of ironies. Bly identifies Dickey with the "average American"—an image Dickey had cultivated in opposition to the elitism of poets like T. S. Eliot. In other words, Dickey, who had presented himself and been received as a bold new voice who would shake up the literary establishment, became the embodiment of the WASP establishment. The "standard middle-class" stance for which Bly vilifies Dickey is the same antiacademic honesty for which critics had once praised him. Bly himself provides the best example of this reversal. In 1964 Bly had praised Dickey's war poems, insisting Dickey's "courage is so great" that "he does not fill" his poems "with phony Greek heroes as disguises, but instead places himself in front of the poem, under clear glass, where you can see him for good or bad."[14] But as the United States became the enemy of the New Left literary establishment, Dickey, who had assumed a Whitmanesque stance as a people's poet, became a symbol of middle-class prejudices. The "democratic" poet became the poet of the "ugly American."

Anthony Libby called Dickey a "poet of ultimate violence" and a "reptile brain," asserting that Vietnam had "solidified Dickey's conservatism, his sense that powerful countries, like great men, are

13. "Buckdancer's Choice," 75, 78–79.
14. "Work of James Dickey," 57.

unnecessarily weakened by extreme moral self-consciousness."
Fredric Jameson wrote that Dickey's work was "repellent" and
"right-wing." Ralph J. Mills declared that Dickey's poems had sunk
into a "moral abyss," reflecting "an obsession with power and the
imposition of will—and a total insensitivity to the persons who are
the objects of this indulgence." Anthony Thwaite asserted that in
Dickey's work the "world that lies outside might as well not exist
for all the notice that is taken of it," complaining that Dickey took
no notice that "a real and bloody war is going on." Thwaite insisted
that because in *Deliverance* Dickey shows "Southern hicks behave
badly and inscrutably; so, by extension, do oriental gooks." Martin
Dodsworth claimed that unlike

> decent men like Robert Bly, James Dickey is the poet of [another]
> America, which can afford to hunt, shoot and fish expensively—
> cleaned limbed son of Atlanta, Georgia, veteran of the Korean war
> and the war before that, who has not yet written a poem about
> baseball but probably will. . . . His poems subscribe heavily to the
> fantasy of a man's world—war, savage nature, bloody sex—and
> don't have much to do with people.[15]

This negative reaction was not due, however, to a change in the
thematic content of Dickey's work, as Bly and others claimed. As I
have shown, violence and war themes were prevalent components
in Dickey's work from the start, and he continues to write poetry
and prose that, without making explicit moral judgments, explores
what violent situations reveal about the human condition. What
Vietnam did change was the literary establishment's and the aca-
demic community's attitude about war, and, more generally, all
forms of violence.

The way in which Bly reads "The Firebombing" demonstrates the
extent to which the Vietnam milieu shaped and distorted his per-
ception of the poem, and it also suggests how the war pushed many
critics toward didactic assessments of literature. Bly claims that in
the poem the "civilian population of Asia" is treated as an object of

15. Libby, "Fire and Light: Four Poets to the End and Beyond," 121; Jameson, "The
Great American Hunter or Ideological Content in the Novel," 181; Mills, "The Poetry
of James Dickey," 238, 240–41; Thwaite, "Out of Bondage," 311; Dodsworth, "To-
wards the Baseball Poem," 842.

"sadism," and that the poem "makes no real criticism of the American habit of firebombing Asians." Bly feels the poem shows "an obsession with power," and that it "emphasizes the picturesque quality of firebombing . . . the lordly and attractive isolation of the pilot, the spectacular colors unfolding beneath," and a "hideous indifference."[16]

In the poem Dickey does emphasize the feeling of unlimited power the pilot experiences, but for a purpose much different from the one Bly suggests. To Dickey the poem is "about the guilt at the inability to feel guilt." He wants to show that "the detachment one senses when dropping the bombs is the worst evil of all":

> "The Firebombing" is based on a kind of paradox based on the sense of power one has as a pilot of an aircrew dropping bombs. This is a sense of power a person can otherwise never experience. Of course this sensation is humanly reprehensible, but so are many of the human emotions one has. Judged by the general standard, such emotions are reprehensible, but they do happen, and that is the feeling. Then you come back from a war you won, and you're a civilian, and you begin to think about the implications of what you actually did do when you experienced this sense of power and remoteness and godlike vision. And you think of the exercise of authority via the machine that your own government has put at your disposal to do exactly what you did with it. Then you have a family yourself, and you think about those people twenty, thirty, forty years ago—I was dropping those bombs on them. Suppose somebody did that to me? It was no different to them.[17]

Bly reveals his preference for the didactic over the paradoxical when he identifies the poem's opening as its only redeeming section, because it offers "some criticism of the pilot" by showing his "indifference":[18]

> Homeowners unite.
>
> All families lie together, though some are burned alive.
> The others try to feel
> For them. Some can, it is often said.

16. "Buckdancer's Choice," 73–75.
17. "Interview with James Dickey," 122–23.
18. "Buckdancer's Choice," 73.

But even here, Bly's interpretation is off because his insistence on creating binary oppositions (in this case he wants the pilot to be either "good" or "bad") does not allow him to adequately address the poem's dramatic situation: a suburban American trying to confront his inability to feel guilt at having bombed Japanese civilians twenty years ago. The poem is not criticizing the pilot, but exploring his present state of mind and contrasting it with the sensations he experienced as a pilot. The narrator's use of the word *lie* indicates he is looking at his own "safe" existence in the American suburb and seeing it as an illusion. Besides lying together, in the physical and communal sense, domestic life presents the falsehood of civilized safety. The declaration "some are burned alive" indicates that the narrator is comparing his present life with the lives of the Japanese civilians who were firebombed in their homes. When he declares that "some can, it is often said" "feel" for the victims, it is not a criticism of the narrator displaying his "indifference"; instead, these lines show the guilt he cannot feel—guilt at having participated in the bombing—and the guilt he does feel—guilt at not being able to feel guilt for having committed the violent acts.

Dickey continues to stress individual subjective perception, as the narrator begins imaginatively re-creating his own war experience in order to comprehend it and to feel the guilt he senses he must:

> Snap, a bulb is tricked on in the cockpit
>
> And some technical-minded stranger with my hands
> Is sitting in a glass treasure-hole of blue light,
> Having potential fire under the undeodorized arms
> Of his wings, on thin bomb-shackles,
> The "tear-drop-shaped" 300-gallon drop-tanks
> Filled with napalm and gasoline.

Though at first the narrator has difficulty associating his present self with the self he once was ("some technical minded stranger with my hands"), he feels a clear sense of power. The cockpit is a "treasure-hole," and he becomes part of the plane ("his wings").[19] Dickey's decision to equate the man with the machine suggests that

19. See Ross Bennett, "'The Firebombing': A Reappraisal." Bennett discusses how Dickey uses "multiple narrative perspectives" to distinguish the different roles the narrator plays in the poem.

violence is not a product of technology or "progress," but a part of the human animal. Civilization, whose "deodorized" worldview covers up the destructive aspects of existence, has been left behind for an "undeodorized" reality that includes impending violence and destruction. The situation in which he is placed—an "anti-morale" bombing mission—allows these forces to become unleashed.

The narrator flies over the peaceful Japanese countryside, occasionally returning to his present, recalling that "twenty years in the suburbs have not shown me / Which ones were hit and which not." He *wants* to remember so to make the situation real and induce the guilt accompanying that reality. Recalling the calm with which the Japanese civilians live below triggers a vision of his own current life:

> Think of this   think of this
>
> I did not think of my house
> But think of my house now
>
> Where the lawn mower rests on its laurels
> Where the diet exists
> For my own good   where I try to drop
> Twenty years, eating figs in the pantry
> Blinded by each and all
> Of the eye-catching cans that gladly have caught my wife's eye
> . . . .
> But in this half-paid-for pantry
> Among the red lids that screw off
> With an easy half-twist to the left
> And the long drawers crammed with dim spoons,
> I still have charge—secret charge—
> Of the fire developed to cling
> To everything: to golf carts and fingernail
> Scissors as yet unborn   tennis shoes
> Grocery baskets   toy fire engines
> New Buicks stalled by the half-moon
> Shining at midnight on crossroads   green paint
> Of jolly garden tools   red Christmas ribbons:
>
> Not atoms, these, but glue inspired
> By love of country to burn,
> The apotheosis of gelatin.

Dickey uses this ironic vision of suburbia to show how "each and all" of the suburban trappings serve to "blind" the narrator from the horrible destruction in which he participated. He also uses this passage to demonstrate the narrator's realization of his continuing responsibility for the firebombing. Because the narrator cannot see "which ones were hit and which not" when he attempts to imagine firebombing the Japanese, he tries comprehending his actions by bringing the war into the American suburb. He imagines *his* world being firebombed.

The situation's paradoxical nature is again emphasized as the narrator remembers experiencing aesthetic detachment as he watched the bombs burst upon Beppu, consuming civilian homes, "fulfilling / An 'anti-morale' raid":

> Ah, under one's dark arms
> Something strange-scented falls—when those on earth
> Die, there is not even sound;
> One is cool and enthralled in the cockpit,
> Turned blue by the power of beauty,
> In a pale treasure-hole of soft light
> Deep in aesthetic contemplation,
> Seeing the ponds catch fire
> And cast it through ring after ring
> Of land: O death in the middle
> Of acres of inch-deep water!

Beginning this sequence with "Ah" gives the effect that the narrator is experiencing a sense of relaxation and relief. The bombs ("something") seem to fall almost by accident, and they result in an exhilarating sensation. Though the narrator feels that "thinking of it, / The fat on my body should pale," he cannot bring himself to experience genuine remorse. What frightens him is not the destruction he wrought, but his inability to feel guilt at having participated in the civilian massacre:

> It is this detachment,
> The honored aesthetic evil,
> The greatest sense of power in one's life,
> That must be shed in bars, or by whatever
> Means, by starvation
> Visions in well-stocked pantries.

Despite his efforts, he remains "unable / To get down there or see / What really happened." The only thing he can keep doing is try to imagine the atrocities in terms of his current existence:

> But it may be that I could not,
> If I tried, say to any
> Who lived there, deep in my flames: say, in cold
> Grinning sweat, as to another
> Of these homeowners who are always curving
> Near me down the different-grassed street: say
> As though to the neighbor
> I borrowed the hedge-clippers from
> On the darker-grassed side of the two,
> Come in, my house is yours, come in
> If you can, if you
> Can pass this unfired door. It is that I can imagine
> At the threshold nothing
> With its ears crackling off
> Like powdery leaves,
> Nothing with children of ashes, nothing not
> Amiable, gentle, well-meaning,
> A little nervous for no
> Reason   a little worried   a little too loud
> Or too easygoing   nothing I haven't lived with
> For twenty years, still nothing not as
> American as I am, and proud of it.
>
> Absolution? Sentence? No matter;
> The thing itself is in that.

In contrast to Bly's claim that the poem shows "an obsession with power" and "emphasizes the picturesque quality of firebombing . . . the lordly and attractive isolation of the pilot, the spectacular colors unfolding beneath," and a "hideous indifference," the poem actually shows the hideousness of the indifference the pilot felt—an indifference that, at the work's conclusion, continues to make him suffer and feel guilt. The detachment that warfare can create between one's actions and those actions' consequences is identified as "The honored aesthetic evil." The visionary moment results in the narrator bringing the war into the American suburb, making him feel responsibility for the slaughter of innocent civilians.

In his review of *Buckdancer's Choice,* Bly never mentions that the poem concerns World War II, not the Vietnam War, nor does he distinguish between the Japanese and the Vietnamese. That he simply uses the category "Asians" indicates how the distinction between the two wars is blurred in his reading of the poem. ("The Firebombing," in fact, was completed by 1963, before the Vietnam War received much negative attention in the U.S.) The manner in which he interprets the poem's opening lines, viewing them as a criticism of the pilot, further suggests what triggers his misinterpretation. Bly objects because he thinks the "poem soon drops this complaint" against the pilot. Like Libby, Thwaite, Mills, Jameson, Dodsworth, and others, Bly wants Dickey to engage in didactic moral outbursts. Bly wants "The Firebombing" to condemn war and damn the pilot for having participated in it at all: "If this were a poem scarifying the American conscience for the napalm raids, it would be a noble poem."[20] But Dickey's narrator never questions the war's justness because he assumes that World War II was fought for a legitimate purpose. Dickey's narrator attempts to come to grips with the atrocities he had to commit in a war worth fighting. The experience makes him recognize the violence of which he is capable; the poem enacts an individual trying to comprehend his actions and subsequent emotions.

Dickey's career clearly demonstrates how history changes and determines critical assessments of a poet's work. During the Vietnam era what was once a voice of complex courage became in the minds of many the simple tool of the status quo, as numerous critics were unable or unwilling to go beyond the question of whether or not a poem presented an outright denunciation of war or violence. Dickey's war poems are not revelatory of insensitivity and unconcern but of the way their philosophical underpinnings conflicted with Vietnam-era altruism. Understanding the romantic and existentialist tenets that inform Dickey's poetry are essential to comprehending how his visionary realism was misinterpreted and demonstrates how a writer who unrelentingly pursued insight into deeply distressing and very real situations became a moral monster to the New Left literary establishment.

20. *"Buckdancer's Choice,"* 74.

3

Dickey and the
Academic Canon
A Literary Civil War

James Dickey's career shows us how the Vietnam milieu not only shaped the critical community's responses toward war and violence, but also influenced the different directions literary criticism took in the sixties and seventies. Dickey's admirers focused on such literary virtues of his work as his use of formal experiment, myth, and recurring motifs and themes; his detractors, sensitized by the Vietnam War and the social upheaval of the times, denounced Dickey for the ideological and political positions they detected in his writings. While formalist studies of Dickey's work continue to be published, the "progressive," socially contextual studies, which either completely ignored his role in contemporary literature or gave him brief and very negative attention, have been more influential. The vehement scorn many critics expressed for

Dickey and the almost fanatical loyalty of his defenders resulted in a literary civil war that has profoundly affected critics' appraisals of Dickey's place in the post–World War II literary canon.

Because the anti–Vietnam War movement served as a rallying point for many poets, critics tend to associate the literary history of the sixties and seventies, including many poets' rebellions against late modernism, with liberal cultural and political agendas that began to gather momentum in the late fifties and the early sixties. Charles Olson, Robert Lowell, Adrienne Rich, Ed Dorn, Denise Levertov, Gary Snyder, Robert Duncan, Robert Creeley, W. S. Merwin, Robert Bly, Allen Ginsberg, and others saw their own struggles in ways convenient to the making of such a literary history, and they implicitly invited the kinds of assessments provided by influential critics—Sherman Paul, James Breslin, Cary Nelson, M. L. Rosenthal, Robert von Hallberg, Charles Altieri, Charles Molesworth, Karl Malkoff, Paul Breslin—whose studies revolve around distinctions between modern and postmodern poets. These studies invariably hinge on contrasts between contemporary writers' "liberal" qualities— ideologically and aesthetically—and their predecessors' "conservatism."[1] But because of the unique qualities of his revolt against the

1. Paul's *Olson's Push* and *The Lost America of Love: Rereading Robert Creeley, Edward Dorn, and Robert Duncan* focus on poets who were active members of the counterculture of the sixties and seventies. The contemporary poets M. L. Rosenthal concentrates on in *The Modern Poetic Sequence: The Genius of Modern Poetry*—Lowell, Plath, Ted Hughes, Ginsberg, and others—are associated with the confessional mode and are presented as "alienated" from their culture—a popular theme in studies that examine representations of "self" in recent poetry. Paul Breslin's insightful *The Psycho-Political Muse: American Poetry since the Fifties* provides a much needed reassessment of many contemporary poets' work. Though his history revolves around the same writers that are included in the other studies I have mentioned, he shows how many contemporary poets' work has come to be overrated, largely for its embracing of radical politics. The work of James Breslin, von Hallberg, Altieri, Molesworth, and Malkoff will be commented on in detail later in the chapter.

Two excellent assessments of recent poetry, which to a significant extent avoid a narrow political focus, are the predominantly formalist studies found in Lynn Keller's *Re-Making It New: Contemporary American Poetry and the Modernist Tradition*, which pairs off specific modernist and contemporary poets, Stevens-Ashbery, Moore-Bishop, Williams-Creely, Auden-Merrill, in an effort to pin down how each contemporary poet's work represents a continuation of and diversion from his or her particular predecessor's work, and Jonathan Holden's *Style and Authenticity in Postmodern Poetry*, which looks at the "analogical impulse behind much contemporary poetic form" (11).

modernists and of his politics (and perceptions of his politics), Dickey has not fit under the critical umbrella of the first wave of books about post–World War II poets. While Dickey is a standard figure in anthologies, and the subject of over a hundred scholarly articles, four collections of essays, three other books, and over thirty dissertations, he is conspicuously absent from recent influential contextual studies.

Indeed, because Dickey has received so much individual attention, his absence from poetic histories written after Vietnam may be read as symptomatic of the forces and assumptions governing the criticism of contemporary poetry. Investigating the reasons for Dickey's absence reveals how recent critics' relatively uniform ideological assumptions have shaped the post–World War II poetic canon. The methodological and ideological consistency of the paradigms these critics use has largely determined which writers receive the most prestigious academic attention. Appraisals of post–World War II poetry have not been able to account satisfactorily for Dickey because the contradictory currents of his career are not easily adaptable to critics' underlying political and social agendas; the result has been either a too simple dismissal of Dickey as a conservative or a complete disregard of his work's social and political implications. What emerges from these cumulative assessments of contemporary American poetry is a perspective that privileges writers' alienation from their own culture.[2] But when viewed in the context of studies dedicated to Dickey's work (all of which concentrate on close, organic readings), such as Richard Calhoun and Robert W. Hill's *James Dickey*, Ronald Baughman's *Understanding James Dickey*, and Robert Kirschten's *James Dickey and the Gentle Ecstasy of Earth*, a deeply divided binary opposition between formal aesthetic criticism and overtly political criticism becomes apparent. Moreover, both perspectives contain profound limitations: one faction risks, by limiting its focus to formal features and supposedly holding an "ideology-free" position, remaining trapped, as Fredric Jameson asserts, in an aesthetic abyss with profound implications; the other risks oversimplification by

---

2. Breslin's *Psycho-Political Muse* is a clear exception. See my comment in note 1 above.

replacing the image of the modernist writer as an elite intellectual with a romantic conception of the contemporary poet as a marginalized social malcontent.

Robert Bly's and others' objections to Dickey's use of violence ignited a widespread reversal of the critical reception of Dickey's work, culminating in many critics' dismissing him as a reactionary conservative. Yet, as I have demonstrated, Dickey was an early proponent of the civil rights movement and a staunch supporter of Eugene McCarthy, facts that raise the issue of why so many critics have been ready to view and portray Dickey as "right wing." Examining critics' reactions to Dickey's subject matter, his southernness, and his popularity with the mass media—all major irritants to his detractors—helps clarify critical assessments of Dickey by demonstrating how his writings and public image often generate turbulent, and sometimes disturbing, messages. The manner in which critics have chosen to read the conflicting signals Dickey's work sends suggests the value system that guides many recent interpretations of literature.

"Slave Quarters" (1965) provides a good example of how Dickey's tendency to see subjectivity in terms of a primitivistic self often gets him into trouble. In the poem, a white southerner fantasizes about liberating his own repressed sexual urges through contact with a female slave, but he eventually realizes that such desires contribute to destroying in others the very thing he desires, freedom from an oppressive society. Though some critics agree with Dickey, who sees the poem as a liberal commentary that "strikes right to the heart of the hypocrisy of slavery and shows some of the pity and terror of it " (SI, 160), others view it as unforgivably racist. Ralph J. Mills called the poem a "sick fantasy" of "warped masculine sexual power," and Robert Bly denounced it as a "fantasy of ownership . . . one of the most repulsive poems written in American literature."[3] A close look at "Slave Quarters" helps account for such radically divergent responses by suggesting the conflicting messages it sends the reader:

3. Mills, "Poetry of James Dickey," 240; Bly, "Buckdancer's Choice," 71.

In the great place the great house is gone from   in the sun
Room, near the kitchen of air   I look across at low walls
Of slave quarters, and feel my imagining loins

Rise with the madness of Owners
To take off the Master's white clothes
And slide all the way into moonlight
Two hundred years old with this moon.
Let me go,

Ablaze with my old me-
scent, in moonlight made by the mind
From the dusk sun, in the yards where my dogs would smell
For once what I totally am,
Flaming up in their brains as the Master
They but dimly had sensed through my clothes: . . .

It is easy to see why Dickey's representation of a racist's con-
sciousness troubled Mills and Bly. Dickey focuses on the white
man's point of view by picturing a contemporary southerner fanta-
sizing about raping a black woman and feeling that such behavior is
somehow natural. The narrator visits the site of a former plantation
and imagines the sensations his forefather experienced during a
midnight "visit" to a slave. He imagines himself moving from the
"sun / Room" and out of "white clothes" into the more "natural"
state of "moonlight." His body, whose smells are no longer covered
up with genteel trappings, becomes alive to the dogs as they smell
his "real" self ("For once what I totally am"). The narrator not only
imagines the sensations of the "Master," but he also attempts to
connect with his own instinctual self through the "moonlight" he
"makes" from his "mind." As the narrator re-creates the slave-
owner's former way of life, he is described reveling ecstatically in
the role of the Master while further emphasizing the naturalness of
his sexual desires:

A coastal islander, proud of his grounds,
His dogs, his spinet
From Savannah, his pale daughters,
His war with the sawgrass, pushed back into
The sea it crawled from. Nearer dark, unseen,
I can begin to dance

> Inside my gabardine suit
> As though I had left my silk nightshirt
>
> In the hall of mahogany, and crept
> To slave quarters to live out
> The secret legend of Owners. Ah, stand up,
> Blond loins, another
> Love is possible! My thin wife would be sleeping
> Or would not mention my absence:
>
>   the moonlight
>
> On these rocks can be picked like cotton
> By a crazed Owner dancing-mad
> With the secret repossession of his body.

This passage plays repressive civilized possession off of the natural. The Master must continually battle the independent natural world, represented by "the sawgrass," in *"his* war," to maintain *"his* grounds," *"his* dogs," *"his* spinet," *"his* pale daughters." He views sexual contact with the slave as a source of physical and spiritual liberation from his "unnatural" life. As the sun sets the narrator can also sense his "real self" surface, as he begins to dance and to imagine himself shedding his gentility, just as the slave owner sheds his "silk nightshirt" in order to leave behind the sterile life represented by the "pale daughter" and "thin wife" so that his "blond loins" can gain "secret repossession of his body." The Master/ narrator attempts to shuck civilized possessions to repossess a part of himself, which like "moonlight," "sawgrass," "crabgrass," and "wind," "lives / Outside of time." This timeless quality consists of nothing less than the urge to assert oneself by sexually dominating others.

However, as the narrator imagines himself as the Master making his way toward the slave's shack he experiences a moment that profoundly changes what he is feeling. He notices a sea gull as it

> Tacks, jibes   then turning the corner
> Of wind, receives himself like a brother
> As he glides down upon his reflection: . . .

At this moment, the narrator also begins to see himself and to recognize the consequences of his sexual fantasy. He then realizes that *his* body "has a color not yet freed," and he begins to imagine the experience from the point of view of his "brother," the slave who is also the son of the narrator's forefather:

not on a horse
I stoop to the soil   working
Gathering   moving to the rhythm of a music
That has crossed the ocean in chains

In the grass the great singing void of slave

Labor about me   the moonlight bringing
Sweat out of my back as though   the sun
Changed skins upon me   some other
Man moving near me on horseback   whom I look in the eyes
Once a day: . . .

Quite contrary to Mills's claim that Dickey dramatizes a narrator who cannot "escape from his diseased view," the narrator does come to realize the destructive consequences of his fantasy. Dickey's narrator, who assumes several roles, is not celebrating the urge to regain contact with basic primitive instincts, as implied by Bly's complaint that the poem "lingers in fantasies of ownership" in which the narrator "sniffs the negro women" (no such passage exists).[4] Instead, by projecting himself into the Master's role, the narrator comes to realize the tragic results of his atavistic desires. Once he comprehends the consequences of his fantasy, he tries to make himself feel responsibility for it by inducing guilt. But in the poem Dickey portrays slaves as emotionally close to animals, a maneuver—appropriation of race—that contemporary critics have come to condemn:

How take on the guilt

Of slavers? How shudder like one who made
Money from buying a people
To work as ghosts
In this blowing solitude?
I only stand here upon shells   dressed poorly

4. Mills, "Poetry of James Dickey," 240. Bly, *"Buckdancer's Choice,"* 71.

For nakedness   poorly
For the dark wrecked hovel of rebirth

Picking my way in thought
To the black room
Where starlight blows off the roof
And the great beasts that died with the minds
Of the first slaves, stand at the door, asking
For death, asking to be
Forgotten: the sadness of elephants
The visionary pain in the heads
Of incredibly poisonous snakes
Lion   wildebeest   giraffe   all purchased also
When one wished only
Labor
          those beasts becoming
For the white man the animals of Eden
Emblems of sexual treasure.

From today's perspective it becomes difficult to read these lines without discomfort, particularly since Western society historically has embraced and promoted the racist view of Africans and Afro-Americans as "lesser-developed." However, Dickey's use of race in the context of Chinua Achebe's influential essay "An Image of Africa: Racism in Conrad's *Heart of Darkness*" demonstrates that Dickey uses this technique much differently from many American and European writers, though he does contribute to a negative stereotype. Achebe asserts that Conrad uses blacks and Africa as "foils" to whites and Europe, that blacks are used to represent the negative or "inhuman" dimension of humanity. He points out that Marlow is terrified by the thought that "civilized" people had "a distant kinship" to Africans, and he claims that this type of attitude pervades Western thought, even to the extent that Albert Schweitzer said, "The African is indeed my brother but my junior brother."[5]

Dickey's poem, however, communicates just the opposite. The narrator's realization that the slave is his brother makes him see the destructiveness and immorality of not granting the slave equal status. Indeed, the white characters operate as foils because for Dickey, unlike Conrad, "primitivism" is not a symptom of inhumanity, inferi-

5. Chinua Achebe, "An Image of Africa: Racism in Conrad's *Heart of Darkness*," 789.

ority, or ignorance, but of authenticity. Dickey's depiction of slaves as emotionally closer to animals than the Master points to the very core of the poem: the narrator becomes aware of the profound conflict of discovering one's own naturalness through killing in others the very thing that one desires. After becoming slaves the blacks become "ghosts"—white, substanceless creatures, as "unnatural" as the Master's "pale daughters" and "thin wife." The blacks' "natural side," represented by the "great beasts," perishes, perversely becoming transformed by the white man into idealized, unnatural "emblems," "animals of Eden"; this idealization suggests the Master/narrator's inability ever truly to regain contact with this lost side of himself. Similarly, the narrator, who observes that he is dressed poorly for "nakedness," realizes that he will never achieve such a "rebirth."

Dickey's equation of primitivism with authenticity and freedom from societal constraints was part of a much larger sixties phenomenon, which found expression in experiments like agrarian based communes and the counterculture's emphasis on the emotional side of human nature over the rational. Two gurus of sixties Dionysian philosophy, Herbert Marcuse and Norman O. Brown, advocated returning to preconscious libidinality by shucking civilization's repressive constraints. Amiri Baraka, in "In Memory of Radio" (1964) and other poems, satirized society's artificiality and its inability to comprehend "love." Like Dickey, Baraka and other writers, black and white, associated Afro-Americans with primitivistic authenticity. In "Black People: This Is Our Destiny" (1969) Baraka declared that positive change would be an emotive, not a rational, process:

> vibration holy nuance beating against
> itself, a rhythm a playing re-understood now by one of the 1st race
> the primitives the first men who evolve again to civilize the
> world.

In "The Primeval Mitosis" from *Soul on Ice* (1968), Eldridge Cleaver stressed that because whites were the victims, as well as the perpetrators, of a technological society, "the blacks, personifying the Body and thereby in closer communion with their biological roots than other Americans, provide the saving link, the bridge between man's biology and man's machines."[6] For Cleaver, and many other Americans, having "soul" meant being in touch with one's fundamental nature; not having soul meant being an overly rational product of white civilization.

Nevertheless, associating blacks with primitivism is troublesome—even when serving as a positive example—because, when considered in a larger cultural context, it still affirms the view of blacks trailing whites on the evolutionary scale. In retrospect, Dickey's and other writers' equation was racist, though it should be recognized that Dickey's emphasis on primitivism has been voiced in a variety of contexts: in *Deliverance* he depicts primitivism through white characters, and in many poems he portrays it through narrators whose race is not specified.

The concluding three stanzas of "Slave Quarters" move from the child's birth through successive generations of descendants condemned to lives of entrapment:

> In nine months she would lie
> With a knife between her teeth to cut the pain
> Of bearing
> A child who belongs in no world   my hair in that boy
> Turned black   my skin
> Darkened by half   his, lightened
> By that half exactly   the beasts of Africa reduced
> To cave shadows flickering on his brow
> As I think of him: a child would rise from that place
> With half my skin.   He could for an instant
> Of every day   when the wind turns   look
> Me in the eyes.   What do you feel when passing
>
> Your blood beyond death
> To another in secret: into
> Another who takes your features   and adds
> A misplaced Africa to them,
> Changing them forever
> As they must live? What happens
> To you, when such a one bears
> You after your death into rings
> Of battling light   a heavyweight champion
> Through the swirling glass of four doors,

6. *Soul on Ice*, 186.

In epauletted coats   into places
Where you learn to wait
On tables   into sitting in all-night cages
Of parking lots   into raising
A sun-sided spade in a gang
Of men on a tar road working
Until the crickets give up?
What happens when the sun goes down

And the white man's loins still stir
In a house of air   still draw him toward
Slave quarters? When Michael's voice is heard
Bending the sail like grass,
The real moon begins to come
Apart on the water
And two hundred years are turned back
On with the headlights of a car?
When you learn that there is no hatred
Like love in the eyes
Of a wholly owned face?   When you think of what
It would be like   what it has been
What it is to look once a day
Into an only
Son's brown, waiting, wholly possessed
Amazing eyes, and not
Acknowledge, but own?

Dickey's point is that the past is responsible for the present, and that the present must remain aware of its responsibility for the past. The process of decline, which began with the Africans losing their "naturalness" by being forced into slavery, is exacerbated by the white man's idealization of the instinctual. As in Faulkner's *Absalom, Absalom!*, forced miscegenation results in the blacks' natural state becoming increasingly "diluted": the first character is put on display and "trapped" in the boxing ring; the next is confined inside "epauletted coats" and buildings where he serves others; the next is caught in "all-night cages" as a parking lot attendant; the final character experiences the ultimate entrapment of imprisonment, as he is sentenced to a road gang; this final phase represents a full circle back to "slavery," forced confinement and obligatory labor. The reality and immediacy of this situation is further emphasized in the last stanza, with a return to the present, as "two hundred years are turned back / On with the headlights of a car," and the narrator moves from asking himself "what / It would be," to "what it has been," to "what it is," realizing not only the past's, but also the present's, responsibility for the type of "possession" that existed, and continues to exist, through other forms of "slavery."

The complex message of "Slave Quarters" is conveyed through fantasies of rape and through racial appropriation, which disturbs many critics, but to label the poem "politically incorrect" is both inaccurate and unproductive. What should be recognized is that Dickey has become caught in a critical changing of the guard, which is accentuated by his tendency to shape his themes according to the primitive, "energized" self he so often expresses through his writing. In "Slave Quarters" Dickey condemns slavery not only because it is immoral, but also because it destroys blacks' and the whites' instinctual side. Dickey's appropriation of race results in a characteristic Dickey theme: the need to liberate a repressed self from civilized conformity.

In the minds of many critics the subject matter of "Slave Quarters" and much of Dickey's work is inseparable from his southern background. Norman Silverstein's acerbic remark that Dickey is "a poet of God and America" who sounds "somewhat like Jason in *The Sound and the Fury*," and Anatole Broyard's declaration that Dickey is simply "too countrified to appreciate T. S. Eliot or Sylvia Plath," is typical of the way critics have construed Dickey's tendency to value the instinctual as a reactionary attitude that dismisses much social and cultural progress as an illusion. Though this is an overly simplistic assessment, many of the things critics have objected to in Dickey's work—his idealization of a "past self," his belief in people's destructive potential, his mystical emphasis, his relative social conservatism—are products of his southern sensibility. As Walter Sullivan points out, Louis Rubin, Robert Heilman, Richard Weaver, Fredrick Hoffman, and many other critics "have told us again and again" that the "traditional southerner . . . believed in the flawed nature of man. . . . He thought the universe to be ordered by a transcendent and in the highest sense mysterious force."[7] Consis-

---

7. Silverstein, "James Dickey's Muscular Eschatology," 259; Broyard, "Dickey's Likes and Dislikes," 37; Sullivan, *A Requiem for the Renaissance: The State of Fiction in the Modern South*, xiv–xv.

tent with this characterization, Dickey "agrees" with John Crowe Ransom "that a sense of evil [is] absolutely *essential* to poetry"; he describes his subject matter as the "mysteriousness or the mystery of existence, which is both magical and terrifying and violent " (*NH*, 254, 226). Though Dickey shuns Christian dogma, basing his "faith" on a belief in the imagination as a source of contact with the instinctual, the world he presents, like Faulkner's, O'Connor's, Tate's, Ransom's, Percy's, and Warren's, is essentially religious and unknowable. Like the agrarians and many other southern writers, Dickey looks to some ideal past from which modern man has fallen, but he replaces the southern agrarians' idealization of a former way of life with the ideal of a former, more "natural" self.

Yet unlike many of his southern predecessors—Wolfe is also an exception—Dickey is not against many of the changes (e.g., increased industrialization and the changing social structure) that have occurred in this century. Dickey recognizes that "you are not going to get penicillin out of a one-mule farm culture," but he also feels that while such advances improve the quality of life, they "can't make life worth saving." He feels that what does make life worth living and provides "any sense of consequence" is contact with one's elemental self.[8] The three major long poems Dickey wrote during the late sixties are a clear indication of this belief. In "The Eye Beaters" (1968) the man watching the blind children at the asylum pummel their eyes with their fists imagines the action must stir their imagination to a vision of the "cave," which allows them, and him, to continue an otherwise inexplicable existence; in "Falling" (1967) the stewardess, realizing that her terrible fate is also a situation available to no other, lets her imagination take over and assumes the qualities of a primitive earth-goddess as she sheds all

---

8. Quoted in the symposium *The Writer and His Tradition*, 23–26. Dickey's description of the effect he wanted to capture through the split-line technique suggests his distrust of rationality: "I envisioned the mind as working by associational fits and starts, jumps, gaps, and the electric leaps across them: in successive shocks, rests, word-bursts, stamp printed or lightning-stamped images, crammed clusters" (*Falling, May Day Sermon, and Other Poems*, viii).

Dickey does not describe mental processes as orderly or "logical" but in terms that suggest "revelation"—"fits," "jumps," "shocks," electric leaps," "word-bursts," "lightning-stamped." He sees "insight" as a matter of instinctual associations that intellectual reasoning disrupts.

her clothing (the trappings of civilization) and caresses herself during the plunge to death; in "May Day Sermon" (1967), one of Dickey's most controversial poems, the Woman Preacher's vision leads to her realization of the primacy of the flesh.

A close look at "May Day Sermon" illustrates how Dickey blends primitivistic pantheism with the southern gothic to endorse women's sexual liberation. But, as in "Slave Quarters," Dickey's means of expression conflicts with current critical values. The narrator, a female preacher, tells the story of a religious zealot who, after discovering his daughter has been sleeping with her boyfriend, drags her naked into the barn, chains her, and whips her while reciting biblical passages. Frenzied and near mad, the Woman Preacher relates the tale through a tidal wave of images from the rural South:

Each year at this time I shall be telling you of the Lord
—Fog, gamecock, snake and neighbor—giving men all the help they
    need
To drag their daughters into barns. Children, I shall be showing you
The fox hide stretched on the door   like a flying squirrel   fly
Open   to show you the dark where the one pole of light is paid out
In spring by the loft, and in it the croker sacks sprawling and shuttling
Themselves into place as it comes   comes   through spiders dead
Drunk on their threads   the hogs' fat bristling   the milk
Snake in the rafters unbending through gnats to touch the last place
Alive on the sun with his tongue   I shall be flickering from my
    mouth
Oil   grease cans   lard cans   nubbins   cobs   night
Coming   floating   each May with night coming I cannot help
Telling you how he hauls her to the centerpole   how the tractor
    moves
Over as he sets his feet and hauls   hauls   ravels her arms and
    hair
In stump chains: Telling: telling of Jehova come and gone
Down on His belly   descending   creek-curving   blowing His
    legs

Like candles, out   putting North Georgia copper on His head
To crawl in under the door in dust red enough to breathe
The breath of Adam into: Children, be brought where she screams and
    begs
To the sacks of corn and coal   to nails   to the swelling ticks
On the near side of mules, for the Lord's own man has found the limp

Rubber that lies in the gulley   the penis-skin like a serpent
Under the weaving willow.

This passage suggests the influence of the southern gothic tradition on Dickey. His "clusters" of words assault the reader through relentless onslaughts of emotionally charged language reminiscent of Faulkner's and Wolfe's prose. Dickey's Woman Preacher speaks in long, sprawling sentences that form hyperbolic and melodramatic masses of language. In this passage, her accumulating declarations of "I shall" are followed by short catalogs of words or phrases that mount in intensity, culminating in the emphatic, urgent outburst, "with night coming I cannot help / Telling you how he hauls her to the centerpole." Dickey's catalogs, like many of Faulkner's and Wolfe's sentences, are overloaded with rhythmic clusters of words. In each writer's work the clusters build suspense by delaying crucial information—in Dickey's passage we finally learn the father has discovered his daughter has been engaging in sex. These delays impart the feeling that the speaker's message is so psychologically and emotionally convoluted that words can barely contain it. Dickey's emphasis is not so much upon what is revealed as upon giving the message emotional weight through how the message is conveyed.

Such a rhetorical style is characteristic of the southern gothic tradition, resulting in works of extreme emotional impact. Dickey, who wants "to recapture for poetry some of the ground it had lost to the novel and the short story," feels the "whole point of Southern story-telling is that you draw the story out. . . . The length of it is part of the effectiveness" (NH, 100). Dickey uses the "verbal velocity" of the split line to create a melodramatic, exaggerated, sensational impact. Like Faulkner, Wolfe, O'Connor, Caldwell, and Warren, he forges an expressionistic whirl of sex and violence to demonstrate the symbolic and mythic significance of characters and situations. His characters, like these other writers', are "excessives"; they are caricatures that serve as expressionistic symbols, not as "realistic" individual portrayals.

In "May Day Sermon" Dickey uses such techniques to present mixed and contradictory images that suggest the paradoxical relationship between Christian values, especially those embodied in southern fundamentalism, and sexual drives. Dickey sees the poem as a commentary on "the malevolent power God has under certain circumstances: that is, when He is controlled and 'interpreted' by people of malevolent tendencies" (*SI*, 183). Dickey expresses this theme by reversing traditional Christian symbols. He describes the female narrator and God in terms of a snake. The "Lord" referred to in the first line gives "men all the help they need / To drag their daughters into barns," suggesting the brutal, sadistically sexual use of God by some in the fundamentalist South. The psychosexual nature of the experience is also indicated by the father's chaining the girl to the "centerpole," the opening of the barn door to show the "pole of light" which "comes   comes," and the "unbending" snake. Sexual associations are also created through the narrator's use of snake imagery to describe God ("Jehova . . . / Down on His belly . . . ") and herself ("flickering from my mouth").

Dickey's stress on revelation, rather than rational thought, as a means of ascertaining truth, indicates how he replaces a Christian ethos with pantheism. Sight, the imagination's ability to see the implications of events beyond one's immediate circumstance in order to find God, becomes the poem's central focus, as it takes on a deeply voyeuristic quality:

abominations
In the sight of the Lord: will hear the Book speak like a father
Gone mad: each year at this time will hear the utmost sound
Of herself, as her lungs cut, one after one, every long track
Spiders have coaxed from their guts   stunned spiders fall
Into Pandemonium   fall   fall   and begin to dance like a girl
On the red clay floor of Hell   she screaming   her father screaming
Scripture   CHAPter and verse   beating it into her with a weeping
Willow branch   the animals stomping   she prancing and climbing
Her hair   beasts shifting from foot to foot about the stormed
Steel of the anvil.

First, the narrator asserts the "Lord" watches the "abominations" the girl's father performs, but as we move deeper into the passage it becomes increasingly clear that the vision is the narrator's. Instead of seeing the "abominations" she claims God witnesses, the narrator sees an orgiastic dance, as the animals "stomp" and the girl "prances." The narrator's observation, "Her hair," does not pertain to the phrase that precedes it or follows it, but suggests the deeply voyeuristic dimension that recounting the experience takes on for her. Like Quentin Compson telling the story of Thomas Sutpen and Charles Bon, she is visualizing the scene, and she is imaginatively possessed by it, not just relating it for the benefit of her audience.

As the girl is beaten she fights against her father and "King James" by experiencing her own vision ("Gnats in the air   they boil   recombine   go mad with striving / To form the face of her lover"), and the Woman Preacher's tone takes on a greater sexual urgency as she describes the father whipping the daughter:

and she knows she was born to hang
In the middle of Gilmer County   to dance, on May Day, with holy
Words all around her   with beasts with insects   O children NOW
In five bags of chicken-feed the torsos of prophets form   writhe
Die out as her freckled flesh   as flesh and the Devil twist and turn
Her body to love   cram her mouth with defiance   give her words
To battle with the Bible's in the air: she shrieks sweet Jesus and God
I'm glad   O my God-darling   O lover   O angel-stud   dear
      heart
Of life put it in me   *give*   you're killing   KILLING
. . . .
to hear her say again   O again   YOU CAN BEAT ME TO DEATH
And I'll still be glad: . . .

Here Dickey uses the vision of the girl's lover, which is generated through her dance with the animals and the gnats, to give her the power to transform the beating into a vision of a naturalistic god. Though a vision of the "torsos of the prophets" begins to form, it quickly "dies out" as the forces of "flesh and the Devil twist and turn / Her body to love." Her God becomes the sexual urge, "the dear heart of life." Like Christ on the cross refusing to recant, she refuses to deny the god she has just discovered, declaring "YOU CAN BEAT ME TO DEATH / And I'll still be glad." Also like Christ, whose physical suffering on the cross results in a heightened state of spiritual awareness, the girl can "change all / Things for good, by pain." The animals know "they shall be saved . . . as she screams of sin."

Dickey conflates God, her lover, and her father to demonstrate that sexual urges, which from a fundamentalist Christian point of view are inspired by "flesh and the Devil," cannot be extinguished. But he portrays this in a way many critics would find objectionable: rather than choking off her desires, the father's beating awakens her passion all the more intensely. The girl refers to "God-darling" as her "lover" and "angel-stud." Her cry "you're killing" after asking her God and lover to "put it in me" and to "give," like her use of the pronoun "YOU," can be seen as directed to God, the lover and the father. The beating also takes on a sadistic sexual dimension for the Woman Preacher, whose declaration "to hear her say again   O again" is both part of her narrative to the congregation and a call for the beating/lovemaking to continue, becoming a near-masturbatory experience for the Woman Preacher, leading her to ask:

Shall He be the pain in the willow, or the copperhead's kingly riding
In kudzu, growing with vines toward the cows   or the wild face
     working over
A virgin, swarming like gnats   or the grass of the west field, bending
East, to sweep into bags and turn brown   or shall He rise, white on
     white,
From Nickajack Creek as a road?

Dickey uses this question to set up the Woman Preacher's revelatory vision of a universe fueled by Dionysian pantheism. In this passage she asks, Is God to be discovered in the father's self-righteous cruelty, or in the lover's deflowering the girl? Is God a deadly snake, or the gentle patterns of seasonal change? Or is He like the "fog taking the soul from the body of water," the mysterious essence of all things? As God is pain and pleasure for the Woman Preacher, God is also death ("it is true / That the kudzu advances, its copperheads drunk and tremendous"), birth ("young deer stand half / In existence, munching cornshucks"), and, above all, sex. The Woman Preacher rants that the women of the congregation, like the girl, must every spring awaken to "this lovely other life-pain between the thighs." The girl has suffered her father's beating so that other women can "take / the pain they were born for." In other words, the Woman Preacher claims women must discover God in the natural, passionate ache of love and giving birth, which springs from the "earth" and is part of the continuing process of life, leaving the world "uninjured" and intact, unlike the pain the father inflicts with a willow branch torn from a tree.

The Woman Preacher proceeds to present a male fantasy of women's perceptions and desires as she glorifies the phallus by demanding that the congregation "understand about men and sheaths":

About nakedness: understand how butterflies, amazed, pass out
Of their natal silks   how the tight snake takes a great
   breath   bursts
Through himself and leaves himself behind   how a man casts finally
Off everything that shields him from another   beholds his loins
Shine with his children forever   burn with the very juice
Of resurrection: such shining is how the spring creek comes
Forth from its sunken rocks   it is how the trout foams and turns on
Himself   heads upstream, breathing mist like water, for the cold
Mountain of his birth   flowing.

Like his depiction of the girl's sexual response to the beating, the manner in which Dickey presents the Woman Preacher's call for sexual liberation is undoubtedly objectionable to many feminists. Dickey fashions images of process, movement, and "flowing," picturing existence as a constantly evolving cycle, in which male sexuality provides the impetus, "the very juice of resurrection." The poem concludes with the girl murdering her father by driving an ice-pick between his eyes, releasing all the animals on the farm, and roaring off with her lover on a motorcycle. The girl and her lover follow no man-made road or track but disappear on the "road of mist," which moves through and envelopes all nature, and they can be heard returning each spring as a reminder of the primacy of the physical forces of the flesh. Like Dickey's other split-line works, "May Day Sermon" takes on a timeless mythic dimension: the Woman Preacher must tell the story at the same time each year; the girl and her lover return each spring to symbolize the fecundity of all nature. This mythic vision inspires the Woman Preacher to urge the congregation to leave "God's farm," find their lovers, and go to "Hell"—that is, experience the natural world of physical drives, which she feels the Bible condemns.

"May Day Sermon" suggests a variety of reasons critics have been antagonistic toward Dickey. Dickey's dramatic situations, often troubling in themselves to critics, boldly assert a natural philosophy that sharply contrasts with the socially and personally self-conscious poetry many contemporary academics value. His emphasis on direct response made critics feel he did not possess the type of self-reflection necessary to question his worldview, a suspicion often reinforced by Dickey's own statements. For instance, he has claimed that the "human mind is dying of subtlety. What it needs is force"; "writers simply cannot understand . . . that overrefinement of the sensibility leads the animal man off into sterility and inconsequentiality" (S, 85, 60). Such statements have generated attacks like Michael Mesic's complaint that "Dickey never audibly questions the values of the cult of masculinity: physical strength and health, unswerving determination, and above all success, be it sexual, financial or otherwise."[9]

Critics' disapproval increased when Dickey lashed out against them because he felt that he was being unfairly attacked by having "had the right-wing monkey put on my back." He asserted, "I'm not right wing; I'm not left wing; I'm not any wing," and complained that critics failed to acknowledge his work for Eugene McCarthy but were willing to focus on his friendship with William Buckley "because that gives them an automatic put-down."[10] Dickey assumed a me-against-them attitude toward the "New York literary bohemia," commenting that "I dislike them, and visa versa" (NH, 146).

Dickey's affection for the South and his discomfort with aspects of the counterculture further contributed to critics' regarding him as a reactionary. His comments on a panel discussion at the Southern Literary Festival at the University of Tennessee in 1969 are representative of his preference for the South over regions that were bastions of the counterculture. At one point in the discussion, Dickey declared that he "thanks god" he has returned to the South "after having been in Portland, Oregon and California. . . . They have a kind of cultural anarchy in California that was absolutely appalling to me and ridiculous. . . . They really are free out there, you know. . . . But so what? After freedom, what?" Dickey then invokes

---

9. "A Note on James Dickey," 145, 146.
10. "James Dickey," interview in Writers at Work, 211–12.

Donald Davidson's argument in *The Attack on Leviathan* for the pres-
ervation of the South's traditional folkways in order to resist the
increasing trend toward a unified American mass culture. He goes
on to laud traditional southern folk music, complains about the
"debased kind" of folk music "Bob Dylan and these people play,"
and tells an extended story in which a father orders his son to find a
man lost in a dangerous part of the woods and the boy unques-
tioningly obeys. Dickey claims that this "kind of obedience and that
kind of trust of the father in the son and the son in the father" is
"beyond praise," implying that, regrettably, in the sixties young
people no longer have this type of respect for their parents.[11] In-
deed, the entire discussion between Dickey and his fellow partici-
pants, Reynolds Price and Cleanth Brooks, focuses on the virtues of
the past and the dissipation of the present.

Like the subject matter of Dickey's poetry and his southernness,
his high public profile also vexed his detractors. Fredric Jameson's
declaration, "What is the matter with Dickey's treatment of these
social terrors is that he is himself possessed by them; he is as un-
aware, as profoundly unconscious, of their shaping presence as are
his readers," typifies how critics have equated Dickey's popularity
with a commitment to the worst of mainstream values.[12]

Despite the disdain of the academic Left, Dickey continued to
receive more media attention than any other American poet. In 1966
Life magazine did a lengthy feature story on Dickey, touting him as
"the unlikeliest poet" and showing photographs of him as a football
player at Clemson, as a track star at Vanderbilt, and as a professor at
the University of Wisconsin. In 1969 *Life* also commissioned him to
write an occasional poem to commemorate the first walk on the
moon. He appeared on national television with the Apollo astro-
nauts and on panels with Carl Sagan, discussing the importance of
the Apollo mission. Between October 1967 and February 1970, the
Atlantic ran three lengthy articles by or about Dickey. *Deliverance*
became an immensely popular book and movie (Dickey wrote the
screenplay). In the early seventies *Playboy, Mademoiselle, Esquire,*
and a host of other magazines published features on Dickey, and he

11. Quoted in *The Writer and His Tradition*, 15–29.
12. "The Great American Hunter," 181, 186.

was named the poetry editor of *Esquire*. He also appeared on talk
shows ranging from William Buckley's *Firing Line* to *Bill Moyers's
Journal* to the *Dick Cavett Show*, and he did a stint as the guest host of
the *Mike Douglas Show* in 1976. Dickey's name even began popping
up in the "People" sections of newspapers and magazines. At one
point, the *New York Times Book Review* reported that he had suffered
a neck injury while riding an elephant in a Ringling Brothers-
Barnum and Bailey circus parade, and *Family Circle* even published
the fried-chicken recipe of Dickey's second wife. During Jimmy
Carter's presidential campaign, the press began presenting Dickey
as "the voice of the South." In 1975 *Newsweek* and *Time* featured his
remarks concerning the importance of a southerner becoming pres-
ident. In an article in *U.S. News and World Report* he stated:

> This country is on a tremendously exciting, creative course which
> is going to hold untold increments of good and release and delight
> for all of us, as a result of the ascendancy of the South and the
> election of Jimmy Carter as President of our benighted repub-
> lic. . . . What we need and have now is a thrust provided by
> Southern ascendancy and its particular brand of kindness, fellow-
> ship, tolerance and easygoingness.

Dickey received more national recognition as a prominent south-
ern artist when Carter named him to read at the inaugural celebra-
tion. Pictures of Dickey reading "The Strength of Fields" at the
Inaugural Gala circulated throughout the national press. Dickey
even became a "Cultural Traveler" for the Carter administration,
giving lectures and readings in Mexico, Western and Eastern Eu-
rope, and the Soviet Union.

The extent of Dickey's appeal among a mass audience in the
South is perhaps best reflected by the coffee-table books he created
in combination with visual artists. Issued on a subscription basis
(largely obtained through *Southern Living* magazine), *Jericho: The
South Beheld, God's Images, Wayfarer*, and *Southern Lights* became
enormous commercial successes. For instance, *Jericho* (1975), which
presents an idealized portrait of the South and its past, was called
"the publishing phenomenon of the year" by the *New Republic*,
which attributed much of its success among "lovers of the South" to
"the name of Dickey on the cover." The first edition of *Jericho*, which

weighed over seven pounds, sold 158,000 copies at sixty dollars each. Oxmoor House became "so flooded with orders that its copies are bogged down in the bindery . . . which can turn out only 2,800 books a day."

In the South Dickey also enjoyed a good deal of academic support. Poet Diane Wakoski points out that Dickey's popularity in the South reached the point of "worship." Wakoski describes a reading Dickey gave at Emory, which the chairman hailed as the "most inspired poetry reading" he had ever heard, and the "entire English department attended." Similarly, poet/critic Neal Bowers writes of a reading Dickey gave at Vanderbilt University in 1968 where "hundreds of people packed an auditorium, many standing against the walls and sitting on the floor below the stage. . . . When Dickey finished, the crowd gave him a standing ovation, didn't want him to leave, and after several encores, mobbed the stage to shake his hand."[13] In the *Southern Literary Journal* (1968), Richard Calhoun, who has staunchly defended Dickey for more than twenty years, praised him as a poet/critic in the tradition of Tate, Ransom, and Jarrell, but with the qualification that Dickey "does not have any of the old critical battles of the Southern critic of the past to fight against the Northern establishment, industrialism, science, and logical positivism."[14]

Yet Dickey was in the midst of a full-scale, well-publicized literary battle with the northern critical establishment and writing poetry that emphasized the need for people to regain contact with their primitive, antirational impulses. Calhoun spends the first portion of his essay "Whatever Happened to the Poet Critic?" trying to demonstrate that charges alleging Dickey is a "hatchet man" as a "Poetry Critic . . . were highly exaggerated," and that "the truth of the matter is that James Dickey finds some good in almost everyone, even in poets he ought not to like."[15] However, anyone who has read Dickey's blistering indictments of his contemporaries in *The Suspect in Poetry* or *Babel to Byzantium* must view Calhoun's claim with skepticism. While Calhoun simply may have been un-

---

13. Wakoski quoted in *Talking Poetry: Conversations in the Workshop with Contemporary Poets*, ed. Lee Bartlett, 252; Bowers, *Poet as Pitchman*, 10.
   14. "Whatever Happened to the Poet Critic?" 75.
   15. Ibid., 75–76.

aware of Dickey's criticisms, a more likely explanation is that he desired to diffuse the escalating tension between Dickey and the critical establishment.

Besides defending Dickey's reputation as a critic, Calhoun took up Dickey's cause in 1969 in the *Tennessee Poetry Journal* by criticizing Robert Bly's denunciations of Dickey. Calhoun also edited a collection of essays on Dickey, which he dedicated "to Jim, for writing poetry in the first place," and *James Dickey*, which he wrote with a colleague at Clemson, Robert W. Hill, is a defense of Dickey against others' "prejudicial passions," "for those of us whose memories of the man include the gracefully intelligent, warm and playful conversations, the spontaneous acts of generosity, and the rare times of vulnerability." As coeditors of the *South Carolina Review*, Calhoun and Hill put together an entire issue featuring poems and essays dedicated to Dickey. In this issue, as well as in other places, the senior generation of southern critics join their younger counterparts in defending Dickey. Hill opens the issue with an editorial essay in which he quotes Allen Tate's declaration that Dickey "is the best poet the South has produced since three members of the Fugitive group—Ransom, Warren and Davidson," and Robert Penn Warren's assertion that he wants to go "on record" as "among Jim's staunchest admirers." Hill acknowledges that they received many negative assessments of Dickey's work for the issue, but neglects to name those who offered their objections. Even more tellingly, none of the essays he and Calhoun chose to publish reflect negatively on Dickey; instead, Hill announces that they are "braving the risks of seeming chauvinistic, sychophantic, or scared [of Dickey]" in order to include "poems written in his honor, and to carry greetings from friends."[16]

In essence Dickey's career became—and remains—a battleground between the advocates of criticism that directly foregrounds political and social issues and those who favor aesthetic criticism that indirectly affirms humanistic values. Charles Molesworth's accusation that Dickey is a "slick hack" and a "hopeless exploiter" because

16. See Calhoun, "On Robert Bly's Protest Poetry" and the dedication to *James Dickey: The Expansive Imagination;* Calhoun and Hill, *James Dickey,* 138–39; Hill, "Editorial," 2–3.

he publishes in popular magazines suggests how critics' political biases have affected their views of Dickey. Despite such claims, Dickey is clearly not a popular poet in the sense that, say, Rod McKuen is. Traditional critics and his peers tend to hold Dickey in high regard: R. W. B. Lewis, Cleanth Brooks, L. S. Dembo, Helen Vendler, Robert Lowell, Marcia Cavell, Elder Olson, Wendell Berry, Linda Wagner, R. V. Cassill, James Wright, Joyce Carol Oates, Karl Shapiro, Diane Wakoski, Susan Ludvingson, William Heyen, Frank Kermode, Philip Rahv, Peter Davison, David Ignatow, X. J. Kennedy, Laurence Lieberman, Carolyn Kizer, John Updike, Howard Nemerov, William Stafford, John Berryman, Richard Howard, Dave Smith, Mary Oliver, James Applewhite, and many others have praised his verse—even Bly has called Dickey "extraordinary."[17]

A brief look at representative assessments of the history of contemporary American poetry helps account for the discrepancy between these differing opinions of Dickey by indicating how recent histories are shaped by relatively uniform assumptions, assumptions that reflect a profound bias against both mainstream Western culture and the New Critical, humanist literary culture in which Dickey stands out favorably. Cary Nelson's *Our First Last Poets* examines how "open forms . . . often signal a desire for freedom from both poetic tradition and social restraint," and the four writers—Kinnell, Duncan, Rich, and Merwin—to whom he dedicates chapters are poets who "experienced Vietnam not merely as an unjust war but as a betrayal of a democratic vision of America and as a negative and seemingly irreversible judgement on the whole of American history." Robert von Hallberg's *American Poetry and Culture, 1945–1980,* despite its claims of eclecticism, concentrates on northern "liberal" culture, stating that the "mainstream was clear: New York was its main channel, and branches flowed to New Haven, Cambridge, Ann Arbor, Madison, Berkeley," and the "cultural poetry" he examines—work by Creeley, Ashbery, Lowell, and Dorn—is markedly liberal politically. James Breslin's *From Modern to Contemporary* centers around literary movements that he views as radical departures—ideologically and formally—from the modernists. As he admits, he "rules out from the start certain writers," one of

17. Bly quoted in "Interview," 59.

whom is Dickey. In *Escape from the Self* Karl Malkoff, concentrating
for the most part on what he views as the two major movements in
contemporary poetry, confessional and projective verse, finds corol-
laries to these trends in contemporary poetry in expressions of the
"cultural imagination," as when Norman O. Brown declares in *Life
against Death*, "'Human consciousness can be liberated from the
paternal (Oedipal) complex only by being liberated from its cultural
derivatives, the paternalistic state and the patriarchal God.'" In
Enlarging the Temple Charles Altieri looks at the "project of post-
modern poets to invent a coherent philosophical system able to
stand as an alternative to the high modernism of Yeats and Eliot . . .
the ways poetry can deal with mythic, historical, and social themes
in order to dramatize the importance of values radically different
from the essential conservatism of the modernists."[18]

Charles Molesworth's *The Fierce Embrace* is perhaps the clearest
example of the ideological program behind histories of contempo-
rary poetry. Molesworth identifies Lowell and Ginsberg as "the best
poets of their generation" because "their fullest voices were achieved
through their ability to make the public events they often deplored
into something like private musings." He praises Ginsberg's "Amer-
ica" for expressing "an embracing, almost a surrendering, irony in
which the contradictory and destructive values of the supercapital-
istic state are mockingly celebrated." He claims, "A greater, more
inclusive sense of what it is like to live in America comes about in
this poem . . . because Ginsberg addresses some other audience
than his fellow poets," and goes on to rail against the "language
pollution" the American system promotes, especially in regard to
the media and politicians.[19]

Molesworth's distinctions between what he does and does not
consider to be an appropriate relationship between a poet and his
or her audience are strictly political. For instance, he chastises Allen
Tate for writing that Robert Bly used his own little magazine, the

18. Nelson, *Our First Last Poets: Vision and History in Contemporary American
Poetry*, x–xi; von Hallberg, *American Poetry and Culture, 1945–1980*, 34–35; Breslin,
From Modern to Contemporary, xv; Malkoff, *Escape from the Self*, 7; Altieri, *Enlarging
the Temple: New Directions in American Poetry*, 16.
19. Molesworth, *The Fierce Embrace: A Study of Contemporary American Poetry*, 37,
7–9.

Sixties, and protests against the Vietnam War, for "self-advertising." Molesworth insists that Bly took such actions out of "simple necessity" because "public language in America is intended to deceive, to foster a false consensus, or to lubricate the gears that mesh induced appetites and shabby products," and he claims that charges of "self-advertising" are irrelevant because "to be public in America is almost by definition to be self-seeking." Yet later in the book Molesworth tells the reader to take heed of "the disheartening case of James Dickey, who authored a book called *The Suspect in Poetry,* a collection of diatribes, parodies, and negative reviews of virtually all his contemporaries," and he criticizes Dickey because "his poems began to appear in such places as *Life* magazine, on such topical items as the Apollo moon-landing."[20]

Like Richard Calhoun's claim that Dickey's poetry reviews "find some good in almost everyone," Molesworth also reveals his own bias by choosing to ignore obvious aspects of *The Suspect in Poetry,* though his purpose is the opposite of Calhoun's. While the first section of Dickey's book is dedicated to scathingly negative assessments of poets whom he considers "suspects," the final two-thirds consists of reviews praising Snyder, Merwin, Kinnell, Stafford, and others. Molesworth commends Bly, Ginsberg, and Lowell for writing on contemporary subjects and for taking a public stand, yet castigates Dickey for writing on "topical items" and for being a "slick hack." The difference is that Molesworth approves of Bly, Lowell, and Ginsberg for addressing "public events they often deplored" and of their anti–Vietnam War poetry because he agrees with their politics, while he disapproves of Dickey because his occasional poem "Apollo" celebrates an event that a "supercapitalistic" state institution supported. He also praises Ginsberg for appealing to an audience "other than his fellow poets" but points to Dickey's publications in popular magazines as part of his "corn-pone crassness."[21] The distinction between the two is that Molesworth approves of a "counterculture" audience, but not of a more "mainstream" one.

The unlikely combination of elitist New Critics and the popular

20. Ibid., 9–10, 80.
21. Ibid., 81.

media holds Dickey in high regard because his work succeeds according to the aesthetic standards the New Critics advocated while remaining accessible to a mass audience (perhaps only Robert Frost has been as successful in these two respects). However, socially oriented contemporary critics scorn his work because they associate him with the "establishment." For instance, the type of primitivism associated with beat writers, such as Snyder or Ginsberg, does not draw critics' ire because their primitivism is used to promote the perspective of the political counterculture. Though Dickey's primitivism, like Snyder's and Ginsberg's, does at times reflect a dissatisfaction with increasing industrialization, his concern is with restoring aggressive, competitive instincts that critics associate with capitalism and patriarchy, as when Michael Mesic claims that he "cannot accept as valid [Dickey's] view of life based on a sad coupling of the assumptions of the entrepreneur, competitive athlete, dominant male, and glory seeker—the hero in contrived heroic situations."[22]

Postmodernist poets' turn away from the symbolist poetics of the New Critics, Eliot, and Yeats, and toward the objectivist aesthetic of Pound and Williams, which emphasizes direct treatment of the topical and the local, has been paralleled by critics who stress the social and ideological rather than the formal and the universal. The New Critics' emphasis on a work of art as autotelic, and their preference for the complex and paradoxical, have been replaced with historical, socially oriented criticism reminiscent of the thirties' *Partisan Review* group (i.e., before it severed its ties with the Communist party), which included Alfred Kazin, Irving Howe, Philip Rahv, Malcom Cowley, and Lionel Trilling. A central reason recent theoretical approaches—deconstruction, Marxism, some psychoanalytic forms of feminism—currently popular among academics have not been widely applied to recent poetry is that the poetry receiving academic attention generally supports the ideological agendas such criticism promotes. Hence, instead of symptomatic readings, criticism of postmodern poetry offers historically oriented explications of poets' rebellions against formal, social, and political tyranny.

Like the stifling aesthetic standards the New Critics advocated, the decidedly far-left impetus behind these recent approaches has

22. "A Note on James Dickey," 145.

imposed rigid boundaries of its own. Rather than presenting a history of contemporary poetry that recognizes various competing trends, critics have identified the break with the "conservatism of the moderns" as occurring at the end of the fifties, and they have created a history compatible with their ideological program. Critical histories of post–World War II poetry view writers through the lens of the Vietnam-Watergate milieu, and have consequently adapted a radical agenda. Dickey and others—Richard Wilbur, Howard Nemerov, William Stafford—who are identified as "conservative," or at least out of step with liberal agendas, have been largely "written out" of post–World War II poetic history, though these poets have achieved a high level of individual prominence.

Though Dickey does retain a relatively traditional conception of gender roles and sees violence to be an inherent part of the human condition, an easy dismissal of Dickey as "right-wing" is a vast oversimplification generated by critics who tend to split writers into opposing groups to reinforce their own positions. Despite the impressions left by the differing critical camps—and Dickey himself—Dickey is neither a right-wing reactionary nor an apolitical craftsman. In fact, Dickey is a maze of contradictions. Though he is a friend of both Eugene McCarthy and William Buckley, politically he is far closer to McCarthy than to Buckley; Dickey's comments to Buckley on *Firing Line* concerning the Vietnam War are helpful:

> A great deal of this has to do with ideological reasons, and a great deal of it also has to do with young men who don't want to get drafted and sent there. I don't blame them; I wouldn't want to be sent there, either. If I were able, or if somebody were able to furnish me with cogent reasons that the involvement in Vietnam does, in fact, keep Communism from our shores; that is from influencing or even dominating the people that I love, I think it would be worth it to have done—to sacrifice 50,000 American lives and untold billions of dollars. But I don't believe that kind of proof is humanly capable of being given. Perhaps it is; if so, I would like to see it. (*NH*, 148)

Though Dickey was not "hawkish" on the war, his reasons for objecting to it were not, like Bly's, Ginsberg's, or Rich's, that he believed the U.S. was acting "imperialistically" or that he was pushing a pacifist or a socialist agenda; instead, Dickey objected because he felt the war was not accomplishing any explicit purpose while wasting lives and money. As his remarks show, he remained staunchly anticommunist. On the same show he defended capitalism, though he qualified his endorsement by acknowledging "one thing about American life" that has "always bothered" him: it is "so tough" on "the people who don't have talent, who don't have drive, who really are not very equipped for competitive life" (158). Dickey also supported Jimmy Carter's candidacy against more conservative opponents. He publicly took a pro–civil rights stand in the fifties, well before he had achieved popularity, and during a time in which for a southerner to do so was tantamount to treason.

Quite clearly, what contemporary critics identify as "liberal" and "conservative" is much different from what these terms mean to the majority of Americans. When viewed in his historical circumstance—a white male raised in the segregated South—Dickey is a "progressive southern liberal," though he may well seem "conservative" relative to the contemporary poets on whom critics have chosen to focus. Though Dickey's worldview is to the "left" of an electorate which, with the exception of Carter and Clinton, has chosen the more conservative candidate in every national election since Vietnam, it is closer to that of the majority of Americans than the increasingly "leftist" direction the academic and literary communities have taken.

Robert Duncan's assessment of Dickey points to some of the difficulties critics have had in assessing him: "He is a Madison Avenue career-maker. And very successful at it. We have had a lot of Madison Avenue career-makers. Yet this is the first one who is actually a poet at times. But he is not a poet who makes me feel happy. I realize there is no conversation I could have with Dickey. Not only did I not have one, but I couldn't even have one in my imagination. But still, his work is very significant."[23]

Instead of fitting contemporary critics' image of "poet as marginalized social malcontent," which, through its own form of elitism views the "establishment" and mass appeal as incompatible with the poetic enterprise, in Dickey we have a writer who sees no con-

---

23. Duncan quoted in Ekbert Fass, *Towards a New American Poetics: Essays and Interviews,* 75–76.

tradiction between commercial acceptance and poetic integrity. He sometimes engages in ventures, such as the coffee-table books, which are primarily intended as commercial enterprises, as well as projects, like the *Puella* experiment (1982), which are primarily artistic ventures, but, most often, he tries to merge artistic and commercial success. Like Duncan, many critics have trouble comprehending Dickey because of such qualities; however, unlike Duncan and other poets, socially oriented critics are unwilling, or unable, to offer a more objective assessment of Dickey's writing.

4

Assessing the Savage Ideal

In *The Mind of the South*, W. J. Cash uses the phrase "the savage ideal" to identify the "romantic and hedonistic" qualities that he thinks are central to southern thought. Since Cash's definition of this tendency has had widespread influence, and because it provides an excellent context for comprehending how Dickey's admirers and detractors have viewed Dickey's relationship to romanticism, it is worth quoting at length:

> Let him escape a little from this struggle [to satisfy basic necessities], and the true tenor of his nature promptly appears: he stands before us, has always stood before us in such circumstances, as a romantic and a hedonist. And this, indeed, inheres in the very terms of the equation. To say that he is simple is to say in effect that he necessarily lacks the complexity of mind, the knowledge, and, above all, the habit of skepticism essential to any generally realistic attitude. It is to say that he is inevitably driven back upon imagination, that his world construction is bound to be mainly a product of fantasy, and that his credulity is limited only by his capacity for conjuring up the unbelievable. And it is to say also

that he is a child-man, that the primitive stuff of humanity lies
very close to the surface in him, that he likes to play, to expand his
ego, his senses, his emotions, that he will accept what pleases him
and reject what does not, and that in general he will prefer the
extravagant, the flashing, and the brightly colored—in a word,
that he displays the whole catalogue of qualities we mean by
romanticism and hedonism.[1]

Cash's words help explain many critics' propensity to view vision-
ary moments in Dickey's poetry as egotistical self-aggrandizement.
As I have illustrated, Dickey's detractors claim that his bourgeois
sensibility results in socially irresponsible poetry that advocates
hedonism and violence. His emphasis on "intuitive reaction" and
on the poet as a maker of new realities is often construed as symp-
tomatic of an unreflective, sensationalistic willingness to ignore
social realities. To such critics, Dickey represents the reactionary
escapism of the plantation novel, laminated with a myopic glori-
fication of the self. Conversely, his advocates hail him as a modern-
day transcendentalist, a poet who celebrates life-affirming instincts.[2]
The titles of two collections of essays on Dickey, *The Expansive Imag-
ination* and *The Imagination as Glory*, suggest how his supporters
interpret what Cash calls "a capacity for conjuring up the unbeliev-
able" as Dickey's ability to surge beyond mundane constraints.
They feel Dickey's use of the fantastic brings him closer to a more
fundamental reality—"the primitive stuff of humanity."

Neither viewpoint can account for the Dickey oeuvre and its
ideological implications, though each view can be supported by
focusing on individual pieces. As I will show, Dickey's current criti-
cal reputation in many ways parallels William Faulkner's in the
1930s, when many Marxist and neo-Marxist critics identified Faulk-
ner as socially irresponsible, in contrast to Dos Passos, Steinbeck,
Farrell, Gold, Odets, and others. Like Faulkner, Dickey has been

1. *The Mind of the South*, 45.
2. Three studies are exceptions to this: Oates's "Out of the Stone, into the Flesh,"
Peggy Goodman Endel's "Dickey, Dante, and the Demonic: Reassessing *Deliver-
ance*," and Robert Kirschten's *James Dickey and the Gentle Ecstasy of Earth: A Reading of
the Poems* all recognize the tension created in Dickey's work by antiromantic
impulses, though none of these studies examine the relationship between Dickey's
use of personae and the practice of writers associated with the primary contempo-
rary poetic movements.

defined according to the criteria critics have identified as charac-
terizing a period. Because confessionalism and other movements
that advocate doing away with persona are regarded as the domi-
nant contemporary poetic modes during much of Dickey's career,
critics tend to associate Dickey with the various personae he has
adapted, though Dickey has written and commented at length about
his use of this technique. Indeed, analysis of Dickey's writings illus-
trates that his poetic practice resembles Pound's, Eliot's, Stevens's,
and other modernists' more than it resembles his contemporaries'.
Rather than relating private experiences and emotions without the
apparent intervention of a persona, Dickey creates a variety of situ-
ations and characters in order to examine the relationship between
romanticism and hedonism, an approach that allows him to pursue
what particular combinations of circumstances yield. But like his
emphasis on the dialectical, his use of persona has led to wide-
spread misconceptions of his work.

Examining critical response to Dickey, and applying his use of
persona to pairs of poems dealing with similar subjects, demon-
strates that when viewed as a whole, Dickey's poetry reveals a
complex process where the "savage ideal"—the relationship be-
tween romanticism and hedonism—is continually assessed *through*
his work, though critics believe they are assessing it *in* his work. A
detailed analysis of *Alnilam* (1987), a novel in which Dickey brings
together his major themes, shows how exploration of this theme
remains the focal point of his artistic vision.

A glance at works detailing contemporary poetry's dominant char-
acteristics helps establish the paradigm through which Dickey's
poems have been viewed. While recognizing the mistake of making
direct, one-to-one correlations between poet and poem, studies of
contemporary poetry affirm Charles Altieri's observation that "con-
temporary poets prefer the direct, the personal," in contrast to "the
traditional modernist emphasis on impersonality," "the use of per-
sona, and a stress on complex and paradoxical statements." In his
influential essay "Contemporary American Poetry: The Radical
Tradition" (1971), A. Poulin, Jr., asserted that in recent poetry the
"speaker of the poem and the poet often seem to be one and the
same, an indivisible person; the subject of a poem often seems to be

the poet's own—at times intimate—experiences, which the poet seemingly does not seek to present as anything other than personal experience." In 1980 Jerome Mazzaro claimed that recent poets "use language and self-definition . . . as the basis of identity."[3] In the most influential history of post–World War II poetry yet written, *From Modern to Contemporary* (1984), James Breslin identified five modes of contemporary poetry, all representing an active revolt against the modernist's conception of poetic impersonality. Indeed, so many well-known studies—M. L. Rosenthal's *The New Poets*, Paul Carroll's *The Poem in Its Skin*, Kenneth Rexroth's *The Alternate Society*, Richard Howard's *Alone with America*, Ralph J. Mills's *The Cry of the Human*, Egbert Fass's *Towards a New American Poetics*—have made this claim that it is accepted as commonplace.

There has been widespread agreement about Dickey's membership in the poetic "cult of personality" that spawned in the late fifties and into the sixties, though many critics have expressed that the personal element in Dickey's writing results in little more than self-aggrandizement. Harry Williams complains that Dickey's work is "a vision parading personality." David Young claims that "Dickey pursues what we might call the poetry of the swollen ego pretty relentlessly" and believed this is "an indication of the fundamental weakness of what is called 'confessional' poetry." In an article focusing on Dickey's collection *Poems, 1957–1967*, Michael Mesic remarks: "Again, I wonder about the personality behind the lines. One has very little choice when confronted with the confessional, or quasi-confessional poems of our era, but to react to the personality as well as the poetry. Dickey seems to feel that his existence is threatened on all sides."[4]

Even critics who value Dickey's work emphasize "personality" and "confession." In *Creation's Very Self: On the Personal Element in Recent American Poetry* (1969), Ralph J. Mills groups Dickey with the "Beat poets, the Projectivists, the confessional poets, and what is

---

3. Altieri, "From Symbolist Thought to Immanence: The Logic of Postmodern Poetics," 605; Poulin, "Contemporary American Poetry: The Radical Tradition," 687; Mazzaro, *Postmodern American Poetry*, viii.

4. Williams, *The Edge Is What I Have: Theodore Roethke and After*, 201; Young, "The Bite of the Muskrat: Judging Contemporary Poetry, 130; Mesic, "A Note on James Dickey," 147.

often called a new Surrealism of the unconscious" (i.e., New York and deep image poets) as writers who "oppose the view handed down from Eliot and the New Criticism that poetry and the emotions it conveys are, or should be, impersonal, and that an author's personality and life are to be excluded from his writing." Paul Carroll insists that Dickey's poetry "explores feelings and memories of one man existing in his own flesh and bone." Karl Malkoff feels that Dickey's work reminds one "of Sylvia Plath's insistent facing of the unbearable, with the crucial difference that Dickey is somehow able to bear it." Arthur Gordon Van Ness claims that "Dickey's poetics, his aesthetic sensibility, resides in his belief that the individual can know nothing about physical reality except through what he himself experiences"; therefore, "one must partly understand Dickey himself if one is to grasp, at least in part, Dickey's own poetry."[5]

Though critics do not directly equate Dickey with each of his poems' narrators (this would be absurd, for Dickey has written poems from animals' perspectives), they characteristically treat individual poems as expressions of Dickey's opinions and personality, without considering the multiple voices that constitute his canon. Even writers who address Dickey's use of persona return to their perceptions of his personality, which in turn causes them to misconstrue Dickey's poetry and method. Galway Kinnell's and Adrienne Rich's remarks indicate how ingrained the values of confessional poetry have become. Kinnell writes that he admires "James Dickey for exposing the firebomber within himself— particularly since the firebomber does appear to be a central part of Dickey's makeup," but he denounces Dickey because he believes that Dickey's use of persona does not allow him to "explore" the "region in himself" that "takes aesthetic pleasure in killing. . . . We don't ask that he suppress the firebomber within; on the contrary, we want him to find out what it means in his own life." In a response to Kinnell's article, Adrienne Rich agrees with this opinion of Dickey, claiming that Dickey "has neglected the real exploration of self, the

5. Mills, *Creation's Very Self: On the Personal Element in Recent American Poetry*, 4; Carroll, "James Dickey as Critic," 86; Malkoff, *Crowell's Handbook of Contemporary American Poetry*, 107; Van Ness, "Ritual Magic," 1, 3.

real inward work, which would authenticate the 'I' rather than set up an ideal 'I' or, alternatively, a persona onto whom the poet can unload anything in himself which he rejects."[6] Unlike many critics, Kinnell and Rich address Dickey's use of persona, but they each feel that this technique signals a lack of "authenticity."

Kinnell's, Rich's, and others' criteria for poetic quality are part of a post–World War II phenomenon, of which Dickey also partakes, but in a manner different from what these critics suppose. While confessionalism and the other dominant contemporary poetic modes have been correctly regarded as revolts against late modernism, they also reflect a rebellion against mass culture. Ginsberg, Bly, Rich, Kinnell, Olson, Creeley, and Duncan were revolting not only against Eliot, and later, Vietnam, but also against a commercial culture that they felt was somehow repressing what was "real," a sentiment they shared with their primary audience, relatively young people who were part of, or at least sympathetic with, the New Left counterculture. Instead of philosophical inquiry, learnedness, or adeptness with forms, the new measure of quality became the ability to obliterate persona and/or regard poetry as "authentic self-expression," whether this took the shape of exploring the subconscious, expressing personal trauma or political discontent, or injecting the poet's "breath" into the line.

Dickey's efforts at self-advertising demonstrate how he exploited this phenomenon as a marketing technique, a tactic that contributed to critics' perceptions that Dickey's work is autobiographical, though his poetic practice radically differs from that of poets associated with the dominant contemporary schools. For instance, on the dust jacket of *Drowning with Others* he asserts that "my subject matter is inevitably my own life," yet he has often remarked that "no poet should be so egotistical as to ask the reader to fasten onto his own personality and his own confessions" (*VC,* 246). His declaration at the conclusion of *Babel to Byzantium*—his best-known book of essays—that "what I have always striven for is to find some way to incarnate my best moments" typifies his bold statements directly relating his life-experiences to his poetry. Similar remarks can be

6. Kinnell, "Poetry, Personality, and Death," 207–8; Rich, "Poetry, Personality, and Wholeness," 224–25.

found in *The Suspect in Poetry, Self-Interviews, Sorties, Night Hurdling,* and many interviews. In other words, like his creation of a public image to bring attention to his writing, Dickey employs "confessional advertising" to sell his work, though he disdains such poetry.

The language that Dickey uses to describe his poetic method has also contributed to critics' tendency to interpret Dickey's work through his public image. Dickey has claimed that all poetry is an exploration of personality, and some of Dickey's poems, particularly the war poetry, do stem from actual experiences; however, what needs to be recognized is that when Dickey uses a phrase such as "exploration of personality," he means something dramatically different than when beat, confessional, New York, projectivist, or deep image poets use similar language, a fact that becomes evident when examing "The Self as Agent," Dickey's most detailed explanation of his use of persona. Where poets associated with the dominant contemporary movements tend to view their poetry as intertwined with therapeutic exploration of their individual psyches, in "The Self as Agent" Dickey details a technique that he equates with Keatsian "negative capability." Dickey's statement that he places "a part of himself into certain conditions to see what will come of it in terms of the kind of interaction between personality and the situation he has envisioned," and his claim that a poem's primary purpose "is its capacity to release to us—and release us to—insights that we otherwise assuredly would not have," sounds much like Ginsberg, Bly, Rich, or Olson; however, he goes on to stress that he is "just as likely to attribute to his character traits that are diametrically opposed to those [he] displays during his day-to-day existence"; the poet should "exult in 'negative capability' and can, as Keats says, take as much delight in creating an Iago as an Imogen" (*S*, 159–60). In fact, Dickey equates poetic prowess with the ability to generate a spectrum of characters and situations:

> The better the poet is—Shakespeare, Browning—the more mercurial he will be, and, paradoxically, the more convincing each of his *personae* will be, for he can commit himself to each independently and, as it were, completely. . . . A true poet can write with utter convincingness about "his" career as a sex murderer, and then in the next poem with equal conviction about tenderness and children and self-sacrifice. As Keats says, it is simply that the poet

"has no personality." I would say, rather, that he has a personality large enough to encompass and explore each of the separate, sometimes related, sometimes unrelated, personalities that inhabit him, as they inhabit us all. (S, 160–61)

Dickey's comments concerning his creation of characters and personae provide insight into his method's relationship to confessionalism by illuminating his continuing exploration of the "savage ideal." Though Dickey reverses Keats's assertion that the poet "has no personality," this amounts to little more than a technicality. Like many modernists' emphases on personae or "masks," Dickey creates a spectrum of characters and narrators, a stark contrast to contemporary poets, who typically strive to break down the distance between poet and poem by eliminating persona. Moreover, Dickey's technique provides a key to understanding his ongoing assessment of the savage ideal, for he creates sundry characters and situations in order to pursue the multidimensional relationship between romanticism and hedonism. This relationship is most often played out through characters' attempts to relate the self—particularly its elemental dimensions—to the large rhythms of the universe, a process that he depicts as a necessary, yet potentially destructive, catalyst in individuals' efforts to endow existence with meaning. Yet critics have mistaken Dickey's tendency to work from within his characters ("negative capability"), and his use of "personality" as a means to generate publicity, for a confessional, or pseudoconfessional, method, causing them to remain unaware of this theme and of his continued affinities with modernist techniques.

Examining Dickey's investigation of the savage ideal in two disturbing poems, "The Fiend" and "Falling," indicates how his use of character differs from that of the confessional poets. Though Dickey employs a third-person narrator in both poems, he immerses the reader in the main characters' psyches in order to capture the impulses motivating the characters' actions. The protagonists' embracing of the savage ideal is the common denominator in both poems, but neither the clerk in "The Fiend" nor the stewardess in "Falling" could in any way be confused with each other or with Dickey. Both characters imagine themselves undergoing transformations from an ordinary state to a superhuman condition, enabling them to feel control over their surroundings through sympathetic identification. Once this process begins, the characters view themselves as the locus of their individual existences, with the external world becoming an extension of their egos, but this is where the similarities end. The clerk's search for consequentiality dramatizes the potential destructiveness of this drive, while the stewardess engages in an illusory, yet heroic, attempt to make the end of her life meaningful.

"The Fiend" indicates how Dickey, like many modernists, utilizes a dramatic mode:

He has only to pass by a tree   moodily walking   head down
A worried accountant   not with it   and he is swarming
He is gliding up the underside light of leaves   upfloating
In a seersucker suit   passing window after window of her building.
He finds her at last, chewing gum   talking on the telephone.
The wind sways him softly   comfortably sighing   she must bathe
Or sleep.   She gets up, and he follows her along the branch
Into another room.   She stands there for a moment   and the teddy
    bear
On the bed feels its guts spin as she takes it by the leg and tosses
It off.   She touches one button at her throat, and rigor mortis
Slithers into his pockets, making everything there—keys, pen
and secret love—stand up.

Here Dickey presents the action without authorial interpretation. Instead, he relies on various associations to convey meaning. The first cluster of words, "He has only to pass by a tree," provides insight into the ideas Dickey develops throughout the poem. The "worried accountant"'s transformation into "The Fiend" occurs as a consequence of the character's fundamental nature. Walking by the tree triggers his metamorphosis, as he goes from being "not with it" to "swarming," "gliding," and "upfloating" once he begins to obey his impulses. His sense of harmony with his surroundings and with his basic nature is conveyed through the wind, which "sways him softly," and his instantaneous erotic response to the woman beginning to undress.

As the poem evolves, Dickey stresses the quasi-mystical state the fiend experiences:

He brings from those depths the knife
And flicks it open   it glints on the moon one time   carries

Through the dead walls   making a wormy static on the TV screen.
He parts the swarm of gnats that live excitedly at this perilous level
Parts the rarefied light high windows give out into inhabited trees
Opens his lower body to the moon.   This night the apartments are
    sinking

To ground level   burying their sleepers in the soil   burying all
    floors
But the one where a sullen shopgirl gets ready to take a shower,
Her hair in rigid curlers, and the rest.   When she gives up
Her aqua terry-cloth robe the wind quits in mid-tree   the birds
Freeze to their perches round his head   a purely human light
Comes out of a one-man oak   around her an energy field   she
    stands
Rooted   not turning to anything else   then begins to move like a
    saint
Her stressed nipples rising like things about to crawl off her   as he
    gets
A hold on himself.

This passage emphasizes the fiend's egocentrism: he views him-
self as the world's cynosure, seeing everything as directly related to
his desires. All objects, animate or inanimate—gnats, birds, wind,
tree, the people sleeping—participate in the "sullen shopgirl"'s "sanc-
tification." The gnats "live excitedly," reflecting his sexual arousal.
When the woman takes off her robe the "wind quits" and the "birds /
Freeze." The harmony and connectedness the fiend experiences
between sexuality and violence are conveyed as the knife emerges
from the "depths" where his erection made it "stand up": the knife
becomes an extension of his phallus. He senses that the moonlight's
reflection on the blade has a direct effect on the television in her
apartment, resulting in further stimulation as he "opens his lower
body to the moon." He believes that a light from his body creates
"around her an energy field." Later, after watching the woman
shower, he senses "the tree with him ascending   himself and the
birds all moving / In darkness together   crumbling the bark in
their claws."
    At the poem's conclusion, Dickey stresses the consequences of
such egocentrism by juxtaposing the triviality of the fiend's every-
day existence with the power he experiences while waiting to com-
mit a sexually motivated murder:

Waiting for her now in a green outdated car with a final declaration
Of love   pretending to read   and when she comes and takes down
Her pants, he will casually follow her in   like a door-to-door
   salesman
The god-like movement of trees stiffening with him   the light
Of a hundred favored windows   gone wrong somewhere in his
   glasses
Where his knocked-off panama hat was   in his painfully vanishing
   hair.

Because the fiend can only view existence as an extension of his
own desires, he believes the act he is about to commit is a "declara-
tion / Of love." The balding man with the "outdated car" feels
"god-like" when he follows his impulses, but the "worried accoun-
tant"'s egotistical indulgence shows the effects of the savage ideal
"gone wrong."

   In contrast, "Falling," one of Dickey's best-known poems, as-
sesses how romantic egocentricism can positively affect the existen-
tial predicament Dickey's characters often encounter. To create the
poem Dickey drew on a newspaper account of a twenty-nine-year-
old stewardess who fell to her death when the emergency door of
an airplane accidentally opened. Through a third-person narrator,
Dickey imagines her thoughts and sensations as she is swept out of
the plane and is plunging to her death. The stewardess's fall from
the airplane serves as an analogy for an individual's descent through
life, where every moment brings a person closer to the time when
he or she will not exist. This process is depicted as an unavoidable
progression over which a person has little or no control. The ques-
tion the poem implicitly poses is, Since death is an inescapable part
of the human condition, and there is no certainty of an afterlife,
how does one make existence meaningful?

   Like the fiend, the stewardess engages in fantasies that she feels
will allow her to exercise power. Indeed, both "Falling" and "The
Fiend" follow the same structural pattern, beginning by empha-
sizing the central character's everyday occupation and his or her
imagined transformation into someone who can transcend com-
monly accepted human limitations:

The states when they black and out and lie there rolling   when they
   turn

To something transcontinental   move by   drawing moonlight out
   of the great
One-sided stone hung off the starboard wingtip   some sleeper next
   to
An engine is groaning for coffee   and there is faintly coming in
Somewhere the vast beast-whistle of space. In the galley with its racks
Of trays   she rummages for a blanket   and moves in her slim
   tailored
Uniform to pin it over the cry at the top of the door. As though she
   blew

The door down with a silent blast from her lungs   frozen   she is
   black
Out finding herself   with the plane nowhere and her body taking by
   the throat
The undying cry of the void   falling   living   beginning to be
   something
That no one has ever been and lived through   screaming without
   enough air
Still neat   lipsticked   stockinged   girdled by regulation   her
   hat
Still on   her arms and legs in no world.

The dramatic situation in which Dickey places the stewardess
stresses her lack of control over her destiny, as she instantaneously
goes from security and certainty to a state where she is on her
own and facing sure obliteration. After the stewardess is sucked out
into the night sky, she remains bound by the conventions of the
everyday role she performs—"Still neat   lipsticked   stock-
inged   girdled by regulation"—but in a position where those
conventions provide no succor, a dilemma that Dickey portrays as
simultaneously horrifying and exhilarating: she is in the "void
      falling   living   beginning to be something / that no one
has ever been."
   As she discovers that she can maneuver her body in ways she
had never previously imagined, Dickey emphasizes the control she
begins to imagine:

and yet spaced also strangely
With utter placid rightness on thin air   taking her time   she holds
   it

In many places   and now, still thousands of feet from her death she
    seems
To slow   she develops interest   she turns in her maneuverable body

To watch it. She is hung high up in the overwhelming middle of things
    in her
Self   in low body-whistling wrapped intensely   in all her dark
    dance-weight
Coming down from a marvellous leap   with the delaying,
    dumfounding ease
Of a dream of being drawn   like endless moonlight to the harvest
    soil
Of a central state of one's country.

Dickey uses a series of images from American culture and West-
ern mythology to stress how the stewardess, like the fiend, reaches
a state where she believes that the external world can be subordi-
nated to her ego. During her fall the stewardess deals with her
plight by interpreting it through images that constitute her reality
and represent her only means of understanding existence. Her rec-
ollections of a television show in which one sky diver passes a
parachute to another and of a soft-drink commercial in which a
woman dives into a swimming pool and emerges smiling make her
feel that she can manipulate her fall, discover water, and save her-
self by plunging into it. She thinks that by opening up her "jacket /
By Don Loper" that she can form wings and glide toward water.
Finally, she indulges in the belief that the experience is transforming
her into a fertility goddess, who will awaken the slumbering libidos
of those below:

The farm girls are feeling the goddess in them struggle and rise
    brooding
On the scratch-shining posts of the bed   dreaming of female signs
Of the moon   male blood like iron   of what is really said by the
    moan
Of airliners passing over them at dead of midwest midnight   passing
Over brush fires   burning out in silence on little hills   and will
    wake
To see the woman they should be   struggling on the rooftree to
    become
Stars
. . . .

And breathes like rich farmers counting: will come among them after
Her last superhuman act   the last slow careful passing of her hands
All over her unharmed body   desired by every sleeper in his dream:
Boys finding for the first time their loins filled with heart's blood
Widowed farmers whose hands float under light covers to find
    themselves
Arisen at sunrise   the splendid position of blood unearthly drawn
Toward clouds   all feel something   pass over them as she passes
Her palms over *her* long legs   *her* small breasts   and deeply
    between
Her thighs.

Though she believes she can control her environment by shed-
ding societal constraints—symbolized by peeling off her clothes as
she imagines becoming a goddess—this is yet another role whose
conception emanates from the very culture she feels she is eschew-
ing. Indeed, to emphasize this fact the moment is described with a
phrase right out of Barnum and Bailey: "the greatest thing that ever
came to Kansas." As the narrator informs us, she is still passing
through "all levels of American breath." Just as she is about to hit
the ground, the narrator interrupts the description of her plunge to
assert that the stewardess's thoughts of survival and transformation
are illusions:

the whole earth
Caught her   interrupted her maiden flight   told her how to
    lie   she cannot
Turn   go away   cannot move   cannot slide off it and assume
    another
Position   no sky-diver with any grin could save her   hold her in
    his arms
Plummet with her   unfold above her his wedding silks
        she can no longer
Mark the rain with whirling women that take the place of a dead wife
Or the goddess in Norwegian farm girls.

In sharp contrast to the fiend's romanticism, however, the stew-
ardess's effort to wrench meaning from her existence is pictured as
noble, though, like the fiend's, her thoughts are ultimately illusions.
Indeed, "the whole earth" has "told her how to lie." Yet such illu-
sions are vital because without them the will to exist and to con-

tinue to exert control over life is extinguished. The stewardess is able to live out her life more fully and intensely because she is able to *create* consequentiality. Up to the moment she hits the ground she "tries   tries" to cling to her illusions, but her final two words, "AH, GOD," are deliberately ambiguous, representing both a plea for rescue and the uncertainty of existence after death as they bring the poem abruptly to its end.

"The Fiend" and "Falling" illustrate Dickey's characteristic approach to exploring the relationship between romantic individualism and hedonism. Both poems utilize point of view, character, and plot in a manner more suggestive of Pound, Eliot, Frost, or Jeffers than of the introspective meditations associated with confessional verse. Yet Mary Ellmann treats "Falling" like a personal meditation, castigating him for expressing "an extraordinary concern with the underwear of a woman who has fallen out of a plane" and calling the poem "necrophilic" because "it mourns a vagina rather than a person crashing to the ground."[7] Ellmann's assertion typifies what often generates critical misconceptions of Dickey's work: she does not consider the poem within the context of his work as a whole. Because "Falling" is the only Dickey poem that Ellmann addresses, she lacks the context that would allow her to recognize Dickey's scope and purpose.

Critics' application of a confessional aesthetic (and the New Left political values they have attached to it) to Dickey's work has resulted in a situation reminiscent of William Faulkner's relationship to the critical community in the thirties. Comparing interpretations of Dickey to critiques of Faulkner in the thirties and early forties helps demonstrate how assessments of literature have been, and are, in many respects, historically determined. Like recent critics' use of New Left values, which champion confession and political positioning as the yardsticks of poetic quality, "Old Left" critics— Granville Hicks, Maxwell Geismar, Alfred Kazin, Harry Hartwick, Bernard DeVoto, Oscar Cargill, and others—often expressed moral outrage when they detected no relationship between a text and their own socialist inclinations. Like Dickey, Faulkner was viewed as sensationalistic and amoral. In *The Foreground of American Fiction*

7. *Thinking about Women*, 29.

(1934), Hartwick charged that in Faulkner's writing "there is nothing . . . behind his atrocities. . . . Each gamy detail exists for itself alone, and seems to be designed more to 'thrill' the reader than to awaken his conceptual faculties." To Hartwick, Faulkner's fiction represented little more than a plethora of gratuitous "terror, pain, violence, and degeneration." Hicks claimed that "the ordinary affairs of life are not enough for Faulkner; even the misery and disease born of generations of poverty and ignorance are not adequate themes. . . . Nothing but crime and insanity will satisfy him." DeVoto believed that Faulkner reveled in "the primitive violence of the unconscious mind," which communicated no real value beyond a fascination with "rape, mutilation, castration, incest, patricide, lynching and necrophilia." Geismar thought that Faulkner possessed an "obsessional preoccupation with corpses and decay" and that by focusing "on necrophilia and cannibalism, on misogynists and miscegenation, with . . . murders and their dangling corpses, we are touching on the center of Faulkner's mature work."[8] Because such critics were searching for a specific type of social message in Faulkner's work, and failed to find anything having to do with their political concerns, whether in opposition or support, they were unable to grasp what Faulkner did have to say. Indeed, it was not until after it had become evident that Soviet socialism had resulted in Stalinist totalitarianism that such critics were able to reevaluate Faulkner.

But despite the near collapse of and disillusionment with the far Left (outside of the university), widespread reevaluation of Dickey's writings may be some time in coming because of the intense political divisions in today's academy. The battle between the culturally and theoretically leftist Modern Language Association and the staunchly right-wing National Association of Scholars typifies a profession that has become increasingly doctrinal and disputatious. A small sampling of recent "scholarly exchanges" helps make the point. Professors Sandra Gilbert and Susan Gubar accuse the distinguished Harvard professor Helen Vendler of sexist "repression,"

8. Hartwick, *The Foreground of American Fiction*, 161, 165; Granville Hicks, *The Great Tradition: An Interpretation of American Literature since the Civil War*, 266; DeVoto, "Witchcraft in Mississippi," 14; Geismar, *Writers in Crisis: The American Novel, 1925–1940*, 163.

claiming that her review of their feminist critique of literary history "demonstrates" how "zealotry turns into bigotry when a blindness to such disturbing categories of analysis as gender (or race or class) replaces insight into what might be the function of criticism at the present time." Susan Schweik feels that the literary canon must be changed because "American culture already works on us as a compulsory chapel of racism." Elizabeth Young-Bruehl claims that "one of the principle achievements" of the feminist Left is personalizing criticism so that the critic's "story of oppression, of marginalization and struggle, is part of [her] work; my story has given me the means to my work and constitutes my special insight, especially the ways of the enemies—sexism, racism, classism, all forms of prejudice." Arthur Krystal, reviewing the revisionist *Columbia History of the American Novel,* comments that "by and large" its authors "write as if engaged in some desperate insurrection; their language is didactic, moralizing. . . . They're so busy firing off every politically correct gun in their arsenals that most end up shooting themselves in the foot." Camille Paglia fumes that "today's academic leftists are strutting wannabes, timorous nerds who missed the 60's while they were grade-grubbing in the library and brown-nosing senior faculty. . . . Lacan, Derrida and Foucault are the perfect prophets for the weak, anxious academic personalities, trapped in verbal formulas and perenially defeated by circumstance."[9]

This heated environment has helped make Dickey scholarship a potential powder keg. Peter Cooley, the director of Tulane University's creative writing program, recently observed that "many university professors are afraid to teach Dickey nowadays. . . . The only place I'll read 'Sheep Child' is in the privacy of my own home."[10] At the University of Wisconsin, where Dickey had taught and been awarded the National Book Award, a well-known poet and longtime faculty member nominated Dickey for an honorary doctorate but was rebuffed because several feminists fervently objected. Joyce Pair, the editor of the *James Dickey Newsletter,* told me that at a

9. Gilbert and Gubar, "Feminism and Literature: An Exchange," 58; Schweik quoted in Richard Bernstein, "The Rising Hegemony of the Politically Correct," 4; Young-Bruehl, "Pride and Prejudice," 15; Krystal, "Reloading the Canon," 10, 14; Paglia, "Ninnies, Pedants, Tyrants, and Other Academics," 29.
10. Cooley quoted in Robert Morris, "Dueling Dickeys," 21.

recent conference on feminist studies several women asked her if Dickey had "drugged" or "brainwashed" her in order to gain support. After I interviewed for an assistant professorship at a university in 1989, I was told that several faculty members were suspicious of me because I was working on Dickey. Like the confusion that occurred with Faulkner's work, academics' inability to get beyond "poetry as confession and politics" has not allowed them to see the multifaceted dimensions of Dickey's writing.

Puella (1982), one of Dickey's best, yet least-known, books of poetry, demonstrates the shortcomings of approaches that attempt to pigeonhole writers according to contemporary political dictums. Dickey's dedication to the book, "To Deborah—her girlhood, male-imagined," points to his most obvious use of a persona. Assuming the perspective of his second wife, he creates a series of nineteen poems, which portray an adolescent emerging into womanhood. "Doorstep, Lightning, Waif-Dreaming" typifies the collection by presenting a resounding celebration of natural processes, the self's independence, and the strength and power of womanhood. The poem begins with the line, "Who can tell who was born of what?" and proceeds to capture the mystery of creation and self-creation by describing the young woman's thoughts as she watches a thunderstorm unfold from a doorstep:

> Who can tell who was born of what?
> I go sitting on the doorsteps of unknowns
> And ask, and hear nothing
> From the rhythmical ghosts of those others,
> Or from myself while I am there, but only
> The solid shifts of drumming made of heart.
> I come always softly,
> My head full of lingering off-prints
>
> Of lightning—vital, engendering blank,
> The interim spraddling crack   the crowning rollback
> Whited-out *ex nihilo*
>   and I am as good as appearing
> The other time: . . .

The young woman, who seeks to comprehend her own essence, cannot discover her identity from "others," or from her relationship with other humans ("Or from myself while I am there"), but must look to her relationship with the natural world. "The solid shifts of drumming made of heart" describe the rumbling of thunder by directly relating it to a person's inner essence. Through acoustically resonant language—"vital, engendering blank / The interim spraddling crack   the crowning rollback/ Whited-out *ex nihilo*"— Dickey describes how the "shifting blasts" of thunder and lightning culminate in the young woman's realization of the vitality within her as she comes to behold her own powers of self-sufficiency:

> I come of a root-system of fire, as it fires
> Point-blank at this hearthstone and doorstep: there is
> A tingling of light-sensitive hairs
> Between me: my clothes flicker
> And glow with it, under the bracketing split
> Of sky, the fasting, saint-hinting glimmer,
> The shifting blasts of echo, relocating,
> And of an orphaning blaze
>
> I have been stressed, and born, and stamped
> Alive on this doorstep.   I believe it between cloud
> And echo, and my own chosen-and-sifted footstep
> Arriving,
>   engendered, endangered, loving
>
> Dangerous, seeking ground.

Here Dickey presents a moving and positive portrait of his narrator grasping her own powers of self-sufficiency through images that defy traditional conceptions of femininity. The narrator comes from "a root-system of fire" that severs her from the domestic domain of the "hearthstone and doorstep." Her self-awareness results in nothing less than complete spiritual independence, as she becomes radiant in the lightning's "saint-hinting glimmer" and "orphaning blaze." Dickey creates an "orphan" who does not need protection and guidance, but basks in self-reliance because she is confident of her power and potential. Indeed, Dickey endows his narrator with some of the same qualities—strength, independence, a visceral connection to the natural world—that, when he presents them from a male perspective, draw critics' ire.

In "Power and Light," from *Falling, May Day Sermon, and Other*

Poems, Dickey again portrays an individual who separates himself from domestic life in order to discover a sense of self-worth, but in this poem Dickey presents this process through the perspective of a male, lower middle-class worker:

> I may even be
> A man, I tell my wife: all day I climb myself
> Bowlegged up those damned poles   rooster-heeled in all
> Kinds of weather   and what is there when I get
> Home? Yes, woman trailing ground-oil
> Like a snail, home is where I climb down,
> And this is the house I pass through on my way
>
> To power and light.
> Going into the basement is slow, but the built-on smell of home
> Beneath home gets better with age   the ground fermenting
> And spilling through the barrel-cracks of plaster   the dark
> Lying on the floor, ready for use   as I crack
> The seal on the bottle   like I tell you it takes
> A man to pour whiskey in the dark   and CLOSE THE DOOR
>   between
>
> The children and me.

Throughout the poem, Dickey immerses himself into the working man's character without using any devices that would readily serve to identify the author's attitude, avoiding, for instance, the type of satirical technique Eliot might employ through an unwitting narrator. Instead, Dickey imagines the worker's viewpoint when describing the effects of the man's home life on his existence, depicting a monotonous cycle of work and domesticity that alienates him from his surroundings, causing the man, who spends his daylight hours ascending to work on lines of communication, to descend into the basement, where he obliterates his reality with whiskey and darkness, before "resurrecting" back into the world the next morning.

In contrast to "Doorstep, Lightning, Waif-Dreaming," "Power and Light" presents macho bravado, in which women and children are seen as emasculating shackles that the man stoically endures with the aid of a few belts of booze. But to only focus on this poem, or others in which Dickey utilizes a similar perspective, in order to characterize his work as a collection of "male boastings," as Jonathan Holden does, means ignoring a substantial amount of Dickey's

work.[11] Dickey's description of the poem's genesis further charac-
terizes his method:

> I thought . . . about the only fellow that I knew who worked for the
> Georgia Power and Light Company. It was my brother-in-law. I
> thought, "Well, what do I know about him? Does he go up on
> those poles? Is he ecstatic about connecting all those high voltage
> lines?" No, no. The only thing that I know about John is that when
> he climbs down off the poles everyday he gets a bottle of Jack
> Daniels Black Label, and he goes home and says a perfunctory
> "Good evening" to his wife, my sister Maybelle, and then he
> retires into the cellar and turns all the lights out and he stays
> down there until he drinks a fifth of that liquor and then about
> three in the morning he staggers up the stairs and has a piece of
> bread in the kitchen and goes to bed. And the next day he goes up
> the poles again. . . . So I eventually got interested in the power and
> light man who got drunk every night in the dark . . . which is
> really supposed to be about a man under these rather peculiar
> conditions who is justifying his own existence by what he does, by
> getting drunk until the profession of lineman becomes kind of an
> ecstatic vision to him and he is able to justify his fate thereby.[12]

The key phrase here is "justifying his own existence," for like "The
Fiend," "Falling," *Deliverance, Alnilam,* "Doorstep, Lightning, Waif-
Dreaming," and most of Dickey's poems, "Power and Light" uses
character or persona to explore an individual's imaginative pursuit
of consequentiality. In "Power and Light," as in *Puella* as a whole,
Dickey draws on the experiences of people he knows, while in
"Falling" and "The Fiend" he draws on media accounts, but in each
case he searches out a particular perspective on which to base a
character whom he then immerses into a specific dramatic situation.

Falling, the last book of poetry Dickey published in the sixties,
details the variety of dramatic personae he uses, as well as the way
in which he uses them. Three poems, "Reincarnation (II)," "Hedge
Life," and "The Head-Aim," are written from the perspective of
animals. Much of the "The Sheep Child" is narrated from the point
of view of a being who is part human and part beast. As in all of his
collections, there are poems—"Power and Light," "The Bee," "Mary

11. Holden, *Style and Authenticity,* 9.
12. "Comments to Accompany *Poems, 1957–1967,*" 14–15.

Sheffield," "The Leap," "False Youth: Two Seasons"—that deal with family life and youth. In this collection, as in his other books, Dickey works from "within" his subject, searching out novel perspectives. Indeed, this technique and reach are among his greatest strengths as a poet. On the few occasions he has deviated from this practice, the results have been discouraging, as is evident in his few flirtations with confessional poetry. The unevenness of *The Eye-Beaters, Blood, Victory, Madness, Buckhead, and Mercy* (1970) stems from Dickey's desire to write "a different kind of poem from the anecdotal narratives of previous books" (*CM*, v). For the first time since the fifties, in the late sixties Dickey was searching for a completely new poetic approach. Though Dickey's poetry had undergone significant changes from his first book, *Into the Stone,* to *Buckdancer's Choice* and *Falling,* his fourth and fifth collections, the progression from tightly constructed narrative-image poems to the split-line block format had followed a recognizable and logical pattern, as Dickey built on his previous techniques, rather than completely abandoning them in search of new forms. In the latter works, Dickey took elements—an emphasis on narrative, myth, mysticism, and a strong rhythmic cadence—from his previous books and pushed them to greater and greater extremes. His release of *Poems, 1957–1967* in effect signals his desire to wrap up this phase of his poetic career.

On March 3, 1970, just after the publication of *The Eye-Beaters,* Dickey wrote to James Wright indicating his desire to explore new ground on the terrain of poetic possibilities:

> It seems to me that the great lesson of Picasso is that he never allowed himself to be trapped in a single style, as so many of our young and not-so-young American poets have done. Anyway, I wanted to move out of what had already been successful for me, if anything has, and do something a little different, and maybe, eventually, a lot different. You have convinced me that I have made at least part of the right move, though while I was writing the book I was quite prepared to have critics say that this book was "disappointing," that it "represented a retrogression," and so on.

Dickey's use of the confessional mode in *The Eye-Beaters* points to one way in which he began to experiment. Dickey's confessional poems differ from his previous work because the choice of subject matter—for example, visiting his childhood home and his high-school friends—reflects his decision to portray specific personal experiences without employing a recognizable persona, resulting in poems similar to Lowell's "Skunk Hour" and "Memories of West Street and Lepke." However, his attempts in this direction fail, partly because Dickey lacks Lowell's wry sense of self-consciousness, but primarily because Dickey is at his best when he surges toward the universal and fundamental, rather than the local and personal. A few lines from "Looking for the Buckhead Boys" point to the problem:

> I go north
> Now, and I can use fifty
> Cents' worth of gas.
> It is Gulf. I pull in and praise the Lord Charlie
> Gates comes out. His blue shirt dazzles
> Like a baton-pass. He squints he looks at me
> Through the goal line. Charlie, Charlie, we have won away from
> We have won at home
> In the last minute. Can you see me? You say
> What I say: where in God
> Almighty have you been all this time? I don't know,
> Charlie. I don't know. But I've come to tell you a secret
> That has to be put into code. Understand what I mean when I say
> To the one man who came back alive
> From the Book of the Dead   To the bravest man
> In Buckhead   to the lime-eyed ghost
> Blue-wavering in the fumes
> Of good Gulf gas, "Fill 'er up."

Because Dickey deals directly with a "common" experience, es-chewing his usual imaginative thrusts, he subdues his language. Instead of the kinetically powerful verse of his best poetry, the language in "Looking for the Buckhead Boys" is flat and unable to charge the dramatic situation with significance. Dickey attempts to build dramatic tension through heightening the moment's impor-tance by conveying what is occurring in the narrator's conscious-ness and contrasting it with what the narrator and Charlie say; but, since Dickey keeps the poem's tone on a conversational plane, the words that he uses to describe the narrator's thoughts are so similar to those used in the dialogue that the moment loses its impact. Where in "Memories of West Street and Lepke" Lowell uses ironic understatement, providing a sharp contrast to the memories—prison, a lobotomized murderer—he is conveying, Dickey's poem remains "ordinary" throughout, never extending beyond mundane sentimentality.

The book also contains a series of poems—"The Place," "Blood," "In the Pocket," "Knock"—that try to capture an exhilarating instant of time—reminiscent of the narrative-image poems—but again, his experiment with conversational language results in poems that are less than compelling. "Knock" describes two people being awakened in the middle of the night:

> Sharing   what sharing   quickly who
> Is outside   in   both you together here
> And unseen out   let the bed huddle and jump
>
> Naked in the quick dead middle
> Of the night, making what is to be
> There   you being broken by something
>
> Open where the door thins out
> Making frames of the room's early-
> warning wood   is the code still
>
> The same can the five fingers
> Of the hand still show against
> Anything? Have they come for us?

This poem illustrates one way in which Dickey tries to develop an emphasis on "connotation and suggestion" in *The Eye-Beaters* (*CM*, v). In "Knock" he depicts the resulting turbulence, but it is never clear why the people in the room should be frightened or disturbed. Dickey does not want his poem "to close down on the subject" (*S*, 57), but since the reader is not provided with a specific motivation for the people's reaction, the poem can only succeed with language gripping and precise enough to convey the emotions Dickey desires to generate. Lines like "you being broken by something / Open where the door thins out," which describe light entering the room through the slightly opened door and falling across one person's body, defuses a potentially compelling image through uninteresting language.

Indeed, most of the poems in this collection suffer from weaknesses that can be largely attributed to Dickey's use of a conversational style; however, in two magnificent pieces, "Pine" and "Turning Away," Dickey experiments with an approach that would eventually result in *The Eagle's Mile* (1990), arguably his finest book of poetry. In sharp contrast to the other works in *The Eye-Beaters*, in "Pine" and "Turning Away" Dickey deemphasizes narrative, as each poem consists of a series of moments connected by a very thin thread: "Pine" presents the "successive apprehensions" of an individual in a pine forest, and "Turning Away" consists of "variations on estrangement" of a man separating from a woman. In these poems Dickey directs his emphasis on "connotation and suggestion" away from the dramatic situation and toward his use of language. Rather than employing simple conversational language, Dickey foregrounds sound, even inventing his own phrases, in order to create acoustical vibrancy, as he does in the first section of "Pine," which, appropriately, addresses the relationship between sound and the imagination:

> Low-cloudly it whistles, changing heads
> On you. How hard to hold and shape head-round.
> So any hard hold
> Now loses; form breathes near. Close to forest-form
> By ear, so landscape is eyelessly
> Sighing through needle-eyes.

Through his use of language and the dramatic situation, Dickey places his emphasis on sound, as the narrator describes looking up into the trees and visually trying to follow the rustling of the wind through the pine needles. The poem's first phrase, "Low-cloudly," signals an attempt to make the wind concrete, but as the narrator swivels his head in order to observe it, he realizes the futility of such an attempt—"So any hard hold / Now loses"—and gives himself over to the fluidity of sound. Like his narrator, Dickey also gives himself over to sound, embracing its resonance while delegating narrative drive to the background. Dickey's ear is concentrating on discovering language that vibrates with the essence of wind and pine, as the narrator gets "Close to forest-form / By ear, so landscape is eyelessly / Sighing through needle-eyes." The narrator is

then "drawn off / the deep end," becoming completely engrossed
in sound, which sparks the imagination, inducing several images,
which progress from the relatively concrete to the abstract:

O drawn off
The deep end, step right up
And be where. It could be a net
Spreading field: mid-whistling crossed with an edge and a life
Guarding sound. Overhead assign the bright and dark
Heels distance-running from all   overdrawing the only sound
Of this sound   sound of a life-mass
Drawn in long lines in the air   unbroken   brother-saving
Sound merely soft
And loudly soft just in time   then nothing and then
Soft   soft and a little caring-for   sift-softening
And soared-to.

The first image the narrator imagines, a net, contains borders ("an
edge and a life / Guarding sound"), and he paints a picture by
envisioning colors and "long lines." But soon the narrator's thoughts
fade from a picture to a conception of "soft." By "sound merely
soft" the narrator does not mean that the wind is blowing at a lower
level of audibility, as the oxymoron in the next line makes clear:
"And loudly soft just in time." Here, "soft" describes a sensation
that is not physical but psychological and emotional; it is a state
of feeling, or *being*, generated by sound, resulting in further ex-
hilaration:

O ankle-wings lightening and fleeing
Brothers sending back for you
To join the air and live right: O justice-scales leaning toward mercy
Wherever. Justice is exciting in the wind
As escape continuing   as an ax hurling
Toward sound and shock. Nothing so just as wind
In its place in low cloud
Of its tree-voice stopped and on-going   footless flight
Sound like brothers coming on as
All-comers coming and fleeing
From ear-you and pine, and all pine.

Thematically and technically, Dickey wants to convey sensations
of limitlessness inspired through sound, as the narrator feels the

wind in the pines taking him away. The declaration "Justice is excit-
ing in the wind / As escape continuing" indicates that Dickey is not
using *Justice* in its conventional sense, but, like his use of *soft*, to
describe an emotive state. Through his heavy emphasis on conso-
nance, especially the use of *s* and soft *c* sounds, he echoes the wind
in the pine; in contrast, he uses harder sounds, particularly in the
final five lines (*t, f, l, p,* and hard *c*), to build a "stop and go" cadence
that accelerates in intensity. The words *sound* and *shock* acoustically
describe an ax whipping through wind toward impact by begin-
ning with soft, continuous sounds that expire with a thud and a
crack (*d, ck*). Having given himself over to sound, the narrator be-
comes nothing but "ear" and "pine." The poem concludes with a
one-word stanza, "Glory," reflecting the narrator's ecstasy when he
is able to merge with the pine forest imaginatively.

As analyzing "Pine" suggests, the foundation of Dickey's poetry
continues to reside in his depiction of the self's desire to experience
consequentiality, a process that he typically presents by creating a
range of narrators and characters. When Dickey rejects the personal
and pursues the universal, he is at his best. (The premise that the
"universal" even exists would, of course, be rejected by much of the
critical Left, revealing yet another way in which Dickey's work is
incompatible with many contemporary critics' ideological assump-
tions.)

"Daughter," from *The Eagle's Mile,* is a hybrid that further serves
to illustrate Dickey's success with the universal over the personal.
The first half is conversational, dealing with a specific personal
event without the use of a persona who can be distinguished from
the author:

> Hospital, and the fathers' room, where light
> Won't look you in the eye. No emergency
> But birth. I sit with the friend, and listen
>
> To the unwounded clock. Indirectly glowing, he is grayer,
> Unshaven as I. We are both old men
> Or nearly. He is innocent. Yet:
> What fathers are waiting to be born
> But myself, whom the friend watches
> With blessed directness? No other man but a worker

With an injured eyeball; his face had been there
When part of an engine flew up.
                              A tall nurse blotted with ink
            And blood goes through. Something written
        On her? Blood of my wife? A doctor with a blanket
    Comes round a blind corner. "Who gets this little girl?"
              I peer into wool: a creature
    Somewhat strangely more than red. Dipped in fire.

    No one speaks. The friend does not stir; he is innocent
                  Again: the child is between
        Me and the man with one eye. We battle in the air,
        Three-eyed, over the new-born. The doctor says,
    "All right, now. Which one of you had a breech baby?"
              All around I look: look at the possible
    Wounded father. He may be losing: he opens his bad eye.
        I half-close one of mine, hoping to win
    Or help. Breech baby. I don't know. I tell my name.
                  Taking the doctor by his arms
Around her, the child of fire moves off. I would give one eye for her

            Already. If she's not mine I'll steal her.
        The doctor comes back. The friend stirs; both our beards
                  Quicken: the doctor is standing
        Over me, saying, "This one's yours."

Like "Looking for the Buckhead Boys," the first half of "Daughter" is primarily plot, a description of events that took place during the birth of Dickey's daughter, Bronwen. Unfortunately, this results in Dickey becoming too much of a "literalist," rather than "a literalist of the imagination," to borrow a distinction from Marianne Moore's poem "Poetry." (Dickey has even told me that the friend with him in the waiting room is Matthew Bruccoli, Dickey's longtime colleague at the University of South Carolina, as well as his literary executor.) Though this portion of the poem does contain a compelling image, the description of the babe as "a creature / Somewhat strangely more than red. Dipped in fire," nothing in it raises the verse to a level higher than a merely amusing account of a father awaiting the delivery of his child. This part of the poem lives and dies with the event. However, in the remainder of the poem, Dickey expands his focus, creating a magnificent and moving conclusion:

It is done: I set my feet
In Heavenly power, and get up. In place of plastic, manned rubber
And wrong light, I say wordlessly
Roll, real God. Roll through us. I shake hands

With the one-eyed man. He has not gained
A child, but may get back his eye; I hope it will return
By summer starlight.
                            The child almost setting
Its wool on fire, I hold it in the first and last power
It came from: that goes on all the time
There is, shunting the glacier, whirling
Whole forests from their tops, moving

Lava, the flowing stone: moving the hand
Of anyone, ever. Child of fire,
Look up. Look up as I lean and mumble you are part
Of flowing stone: understand: you are part of the wave,
                            Of the glacier's irrevocable
Millennial inch.
                            "This is the one," the friend repeats
In his end-of-it daze, his beard gone
Nearly silver, now, with honor, in the all-night night
Of early morning. Godfather, I say

To him: not father of God, but assistant
Father to this one. All forests are moving, all waves,
All lava and ice. I lean. I touch

One finger. Real God, roll.

Roll.

Here the poem's narrator changes from being just another father
in the waiting room to being a prophetic messenger ("I set my feet /
In Heavenly power")—from confessional narrator to imaginative
persona—for in this section of "Daughter" Dickey extends beyond
the level of event, defining the "Real God" as the force that "causes
everything to exist, like the laws of motion."[13] Though the girl's
birth is directly referred to, the primary focus is on showing the
miraculous power "that goes on all the time," connecting human
life with the force that moves glaciers and makes the lava flow. The
child becomes an element—"fire" and "part of the wave"—which is

13. "Interview with James Dickey," 122.

part of the power "moving the hand / Of anyone, ever." Dickey stresses the pantheistic quality of his vision by emphasizing that the Godfather is not "holy" but part of the chain of natural wonders, an "assistant / Father," as the narrator concludes by connecting universal forces, which are "moving" as he leans and touches the babe, to the newest power on the planet.

Alnilam, which Dickey feels is "the only piece of writing I have ever done of which I would say that I would not change a word," provides a good vehicle for evaluating Dickey's continuing assessment of the savage ideal, because in this gargantuan novel he brings together the major concerns of his literary career: "the relationship between sources of power and the imagination."[14] In *Alnilam*, Dickey pits the energized personality, which refuses to give in to "the vast sluggish forces of habit, mechanization and mental torpor," against the structured bureaucracy of the military and, by implication, of society in general ("EM," 165). However, unlike most Vietnam and post–Vietnam era works dealing with similar issues, *Alnilam* does not deal with specific political circumstances. Instead it strains to remain "apolitical" by portraying nonconformity as the imaginative attempt to "energize" life with consequence or meaning. This results in a social meditation played out in terms of Dickey's concerns with the relationship between romantic individualism and hedonism, rather than through particular political issues, making *Alnilam* an appropriate medium for examining the motivations behind Dickey's artistic vision. More specifically, Dickey details how poetry, especially through the image, can—and cannot—serve as a catalyst for self-realization. Where in his poetry Dickey typically limits his exploration of the savage ideal to the perspective of one character per poem, in *Alnilam* he sorts through a variety of perspectives. As with his poetry, no character in the work can be equated with Dickey; however, concepts that Dickey expresses in essays are echoed by various characters, and the novel's plot clearly makes conspicuous the ways in which poetry and romantic impulses can be channeled to energize the individual, creat-

14. Dickey, letter to author, June 20, 1989, and interview with author, August 8–15, 1989.

ing a window to Dickey's distinctions between the drive for con-
sequentiality's positive and negative dimensions.[15] Dickey's por-
trayal of the individualistic impulse to rebel against conformity
demonstrates how Dickey shows the attractions and the dangers of
obfuscating political dissent with romantic idealism by distinguish-
ing between Frank Cahill's and the Alnilam cadets' uses of their
imaginative faculties.

Dickey's thoughts on the energized personality are a key to un-
derstanding his objectives in *Alnilam*. In his essay "The Energized
Man" Dickey describes the "ultimate horror" of living "without
having had more than a fraction of one's own life." He claims that
he is "convinced" contemporary Americans' unhappiness results
from "not using our energies properly . . . in any significant way,"
and that "it is against this sense of inconsequence and fruitless drift
that the poet stands" (164–65). In putting together his portraits of
energized personalities, Dickey endows Frank and Joel Cahill, par-
ticularly in the manner in which the father imaginatively constructs
the world from out of his blindness, with many of the characteris-
tics he associates with the poet. The Cahills' idealization of the
physical/primitive and the imaginative is very similar to the quali-
ties Dickey often seeks and presents in his poetry, and their belief in
the imagination's ability to interact with the physical world to create
a transcendent reality parallels Dickey's own assertions of poetry's
ability to liberate people from stultifying social circumstances.

Frank Cahill, a bearish, hard-drinking, weight-lifting Atlantan, is
a typical masculine Dickey character. The novel's first scenes estab-

---

15. Though critics have discussed the novel's romantic elements, especially the
"energized" or heightened state of awareness the protagonist attains, they have not
recognized what Dickey has characterized as "the horrible destructiveness of such
egotism" (interview with author, August 8–15, 1989). In an issue of the *James Dickey
Newsletter* (Spring 1989) dedicated to *Alnilam*, Gary Kerley claims that by the novel's
conclusion the protagonist, Cahill, "has, in effect, transcended ordinary life and
made the unreal real" ("Unifying the Energy and Balancing the Vision," 23). In the
same issue Robert C. Covel writes, "Frank and Joel Cahill . . . become images of the
Energized man" ("A Starry Place: The Energized Man in *Alnilam*," 8). While both
Frank and Joel Cahill certainly do possess, or come to possess, many of the qualities
Dickey associates with the energized self, what critics have not pointed out is that in
Alnilam Dickey engages in his most complete assessment of the energized person-
ality, detailing the dangers—indeed, the "evil"—potential of such a self, as well as
its positive characteristics.

lish Cahill's egotism, primitivistic urges, and love of independence. Though he is staying in an unfamiliar boardinghouse on his way to Peckover, Cahill, clad in his underwear, ventures outside in the middle of the night to relieve his bladder and empty his bowels. From the locked security of his room, Cahill moves to the unpredictability of the "open." As he finds the stairs and begins to descend he exclaims, "We're winning. Nobody can stand against us" (4). Like an animal marking its territory, once outside he begins "to turn, spraying himself over the white landscape" and is pleased to know that the "snow crackled and burned around him for no reason but his will"; however, in a moment that foreshadows the self-insight he will later attain, he realizes that because of his "willful and senseless spinning—that of a big red-faced man wanting to face all directions the dark could show, and put his mark on it"—he "had lost the house" (5). Using his own feces to reorient himself, he eventually finds his way back, though not before he falls and cuts his head ("It cost us, but we got it"). Back in bed he egotistically exclaims, "You show me . . . anybody else who could'a done what I just did." Touching the drying wound on his head and his penis at the same time, he says, "You ain't never gonna give down. Not now or not ever. None of us" (7).

Here Cahill's egotistical and competitive assertions, and his simultaneous touching of wound and sexual organ, indicate how he defines his masculine self-worth. He idealizes his masculinity in terms of his ability to succeed at and endure physical challenges; however, implicit in this idealization is the fear of failure. Cahill considers "himself a man alone; self-sufficiency and the control of elements of his life were as valuable to him as food" (13); but, blind and sick with a "very bad case" of diabetes, and the "highest fasting sugar" the doctor has "ever seen," he is acutely aware that the "hurricane of sugar" his own body produces may rob him of things he cherishes, such as his physical prowess and the ability to control his own destiny (14).

Ironically, the loss of sight and the physical deterioration Cahill experiences introduce an entirely new dimension to his life. Cahill's conversation with Dr. Ghil, who informs him he will soon be completely blind, suggests the possibilities blindness will open up for Cahill. Ghil tells him he is "headed for the Big Dark, the solution to the universal puzzle," and that "diabetes can be devilish. But if you have the guts, it can help you live longer . . . know more and feel more. What people want in their lives, and almost never have, is meaning. That, the blind have, and it's with them every second" (16).

As the novel progresses, Cahill's blindness does result in the heightened state of awareness Ghil describes, creating the kind of "enormous increase in perception" and "increased ability to understand and interpret the order of one's experience" that Dickey attributes to the energized personality ("EM," 164). Dickey's decision for Cahill to achieve an "increased ability to understand and interpret the order" of his experience through "blindness" indicates that for Dickey the key to discovering and comprehending "meaning" is located in the personal, subjective realm of the imagination, not in the exterior world of social and political realities. (Dickey has often remarked that rather than serving a political and social purpose, great art "involves a deepening of the beholder's personal experience" [VC, 163].) Cahill's eyes only see the outer world of concrete circumstance, suppressing his inner vision, which blindness catalyzes by forcing him to retreat into his own mind. Dickey's portrayal of key scenes through columns of "Dark," the imaginatively fertile world the blind man constructs, and "Light," the world of ordinary sight, further emphasizes this point. However, as Dr. Ghil's statement indicates, an existence where "everything means" may contain a potentially destructive, or "devilish," dimension, as well as a positive side (16).

The line that separates these two realms is suggested when the owner of the boardinghouse in Peckover, Boyd McLendon, plays a practical joke on Cahill. Unable to rely on his eyes, Cahill begins to idealize the imagination's ability for achieving revelation through transforming the physical. McLendon asks Cahill to guess what kind of animal he is holding by feeling the beast's skull. McLendon places a deer's antlers on the head of a wild boar, and tells Cahill the animal is a hybrid, a "wild doar." Though McLendon apologizes for playing the prank on the blind man, Cahill insists that he does not regard it as a joke at all. He claims that blindness has showed him that "everything . . . has got another side to it. . . . You start to put things together in another way. . . . More and more, you come to the notion that you can have the world be anything you want it to be, because it's in your head anyway" (38–39). Cahill qualifies his assertion with the warning that one must "keep on drawin' the line between what you can use and what's liable to hurt you" (39).

Cahill's contention that the "doar has just been made up, and made; he true now" (39), closely echoes Dickey's claim that the poet's function is "not trying to tell the truth, but to make it" (*S*, 156). Dickey consistently describes Cahill's attempts to imagine the exterior world as an effort to "image," and these images are what "make" Cahill's world. When first encountering Cadet Shears, "Cahill imaged him as at least as tall as he, though probably not as heavy, thickset. . . . That would do; from now on that would be Shears" (89). Upon meeting McCaig "Cahill invented him, putting together an image, adding to it, changing it" (106). When Cahill meets Lennox Whitehall he gets "hold of enough of him by his voice to begin to visualize" and feels "it did not matter whether he was wrong, or even if he came close" (151). Similarly, Cahill "images" himself, events, and his surroundings.

Through "imaging," Cahill's blindness leads him into an existence where his everyday actions of constructing the world more and more closely resemble Dickey's own conception of the poetic process:

There was a new principle to his life now. He recognized slowly . . . a sense of complicity developing between him and the concrete as his images, in their locked, endless field, took on qualities they had not shown. Up until now they had been static, more or less like substanceless photographs, bright with primary colors, and meaningful, but unchanging. Now, with the loft of the handkerchief-parachute thrust by the wind—more like being drawn—up the pure string leading into the sky, to the tiny red room of the box overhead, the surge of confident power that results from entering a new dimension, of coming on a new resource, limitless, full of possibility and secret authority, opened everything he knew. Now the coins in the air above the pool at Willow Plunge did not merely hang in the sunlight, bright flecks through which shot the endless gold streaks and smears of his blindness, but fell, and from the four rims of the pool many figures leaped, with much noise, confusedly after them. . . . All memory filled with movement and interest. (172)

Here Cahill experiences a transformation away from the "static" image, and toward what I described in Chapter 1 as the "narrative image." Through such radically subjective narrative images Cahill comes to believe he can control and transform reality and achieve genuine revelation. Cahill considers this "new resource" "limitless," no longer "drawin' the line between what you can use and what is liable to hurt you." Instead, like the handkerchief-parachute being "drawn" to the sky, Cahill is seductively lured by what he believes to be the narrative image's potential for revelation (a point to which I will return).

Dickey uses Frank Cahill's son, Joel, to provide another dimension in his exploration of romantic individualism. Like his father, Joel is a "man's man." Though physically smaller and leaner than his father, he is charismatic, confident, and self-reliant; a superior athlete and a gifted pilot, he is worshipped by many of his fellow cadets. Whitehall, the navigator at the base, describes Joel as the "ultimate male kind of thing, raised to a higher degree. . . . He was more involved with his own mind. . . . He was more willing to go all the way with it, than we were, or than we could. . . . I felt as though I had never seen a human being at absolutely full potential before; at absolutely full potential" (158–59)—a description that closely resembles Dickey's conception of the energized personality as "the man who functions with not, say, fifteen percent of his faculties . . . but, ideally, with a hundred percent" ("EM," 165).

Dickey also connects Joel's theories on and talent for flying with the poetic process. Whitehall tells Cahill that Joel "thrived" on the "mystical part of navigation." He goes on to say that Joel saw all aspects of existence in metaphorical terms, telling Cahill that his son's mind "did not seem to work according to any logical pattern. Everything he said was some kind of comparison or another" (158); for Joel, "navigation was really a form of poetry" (443). Unlike Cadet Bobo ("bobo" is Spanish for "fool"), the "perfect system slave" who is "in the institutional lock" and "flies a pretty fair Link mission" because he follows the instruments and gauges (330), Joel is a "natural" who has "the whole-air feelin'" (111). Joel is able to fly the plane adeptly the first time he enters it, and his instructor states that when he rode with Joel he felt that the "airplane was flyin' itself. . . . Everybody who knew him could tell there was somethin' not real about him, and there was. Not real, but better" (139).

To reach the level where he becomes and discovers the "not real, but better," Joel and his followers recite lines of poetry from James Thomson and Shelley, again strongly suggestive of Dickey's own statements regarding poetry's ability to energize the individual and transform the mundane world into something of greater conse-quence. Like Dickey's claims that in creating images poets "ask each of their readers not to see the poet's tree, but to supply one from his own life" (*MA*, 11), and that poetry "is a happening in depth, rather than at the surface" ("EM," 164), Joel's notes assert that "'through incantation, each thinks he has summoned the words from some deep place in himself that only he knows" (406–7). Recalling Dickey's declarations that "the world, the human mind, is dying of subtlety. What it needs is force" (*S*, 85), and his desire for a "poetry of murderous drives" (*S*, 97), Shears, who assumes leader-ship of Alnilam after Joel's death/disappearance, tells Frank that the cult of "precision mysticism" Joel founded wants "to get rid of all of the usual human characteristics, the things that slow you down, that get in the way, like too much sympathy, too much anal-ysis, too much mind complication. . . . What is sacred is dangerous" (408). Similarly, Harbelis, also echoing Joel, uses the "gibbons mon-key" metaphor to liken flying to a process that closely parallels Dickey's romantic aesthetic in its emphasis on sympathetic identi-fication with one's surroundings: "His whole environment gives itself to him in the rhythm, it flows around him, everything is linked, everything is together for him, and is part of his motion, it's all flow and it's all him, as long as he keeps it up" (331).

Like the killer in "The Fiend," the stewardess in "Falling," Lewis in *Deliverance*, and many of Dickey's characters, Frank Cahill shares his son's need to see himself as the center of all activities, as the one around whom all activities flow. When Cahill arrives at the base and meets Colonel Hoccleave, he thinks, "Beginning right now, I am the center of this thing" (47). Later, he feels "gathering in him the strength he believed he could call on more and more in the sightless realm . . . deep and new-made, with him at the center" (72). He tells himself, "Everything here including the air over it all is an enormous net organized around me; I move, it moves. . . . It all flows in on me. . . . They will come to me, any way I ask" (115), and he feels he must "keep in the center, and keep people and things relating to me" (125). Cahill believes "that his presence at the base was the center of a block of experience fraught with special meanings and significances" (323).

Dickey sets Joel and Frank Cahill's desire to make themselves the "center" against the regulated and structured organization of the military establishment, and, indeed, of society in general. Dickey's stated purpose is to place Frank Cahill's and the cadets' idealism against "the gigantic bureaucracy of the Air Force, and, by extension, the machine bureaucracies against which the kids of today are revolting . . . the social system which makes it possible and even mandatory" (S, 41–42). Whenever confronted with authority Frank Cahill bristles in defiance, disdaining rules and institutions, or any form of governance: he refuses to follow Dr. Ghil's advice to enroll in a school for the blind or purchase a seeing-eye dog; he destroys his marriage through his infidelities, and he is glad to see it dissolve; he threatens the bus driver who attempts to enforce the company policy of "no animals"; and he is repeatedly at odds with Colonel Hoccleave, ignoring his authority, threatening him, breaking camp rules, and finally declaring that he will never have anything to do with the military again. Similarly, Lieutenant Spigner, the "tactical officer for the base," describes Joel as "very unmilitary, very unofficerlike . . . a bad influence on the others. . . . He never paid any particular attention to the letter of the law" (400).

More than any other figure in the novel, Dr. Iannone serves as a foil to Cahill's and the cadets' nonconformity and differing brands of romantic idealism. Iannone, who represents the completely "practical" person, is intelligent, good-humored, caring, articulate, and, though not obsessive about military rules and regulations, follows standard procedure in order to keep the base organized and operating. In distinct contrast to Joel, he detests flying, finds airplanes "entirely rigid," and believes that "the idea of the whole earth tilting up like it does when you turn is so disturbing that, once you've seen it, once you've been on it, you never come back to believing there is any stability in life. . . . I wish I had never been off the ground" (312). He also feels that adolescent immaturity is at the heart of the cadets' endeavor, and he tells the blind man that "boys like to get together in groups and be against. . . . Mostly they want to be themselves, they want to take things in their own way, and interpret them in a way that's like, well, like make-believe. And, yes, I am talking about Joel and his bunch" (311, 310). Near the novel's conclusion, Iannone attributes the formation of Alnilam to Joel's charisma, his "ability to make other people's imagination work," and to the existence of the power the cadets feel they command as a result of flying, which Dickey once again relates to the poetic process—in this instance through an allusion to Emily Dickinson's poem about the unworldly ecstasy poetry makes possible, "I Taste a Liquor Never Brewed": Iannone declares, "When they drink that air coming through that open cockpit they're drinking something more powerful than any liquor ever made" (650).

In short, both Frank and Joel Cahill are presented as idealistic rebels who see the restraints inherent in any organized system as limitations to their ability to live on their own terms and achieve their full potential. Though Dickey clearly sympathizes with their nonconformist impulses, rather than glorifying the way in which their imaginations lead them to an "energized" state, he closely links the tendency to see oneself as the "center" of existence to a destructive form of egotism. (Dickey has remarked, "You would rather be something, even if murder is involved, than nothing. The Lee Harvey Oswalds of the world would rather be murderers than the nothings that they are" [NH, 95].) But in contrast to the cadets, Frank Cahill eventually learns the danger of trying to make the world conform to the demands of his ego.

Where Cahill's idealism involves a personal, Emersonian form of revelation—much like the kind Dickey promotes through his poetry—Joel seeks to replace the current system by creating a new order. The Alnilam cadets explain to Cahill that they want to go "beyond the engine" (408), "fly without the airplane" (340), enter "the purple country," "a field of electricity and a field of flowers. One visible and the other invisible," and "live in a world of nihilism and music. We'll be weightless, in the Second Body, the Old Brain, but still control the ground under our feet" (408–11). Alnilam's members claim "that our main weapon is indifference. Indifference and austerity: to let nothing give us emotion" (433), but their desire to achieve an "egoless," Zen-like state where "the main fact . . . is the emptiness, the nothing of it" is constantly undercut. For instance, when Cahill shows his irritation with Shears's explanation of Joel's theories, Shears is not "indifferent" but has "trouble keeping impatience out of his voice" (433). Cahill asks a series of practical questions ("Now just where is your electricity gonna come from?"), making Shears "stiffen." When another cadet jumps into the conversation Shears is "surprised" and shows "irritation" (412).

That Alnilam's hierarchy is laden with battles between individual egos suggests Dickey's belief in the impossibility of ever escaping egotistical drives. Cadets Willis and Gilbeau want to become members of the group but are rejected by the others. Within the group, Shears's desire to be Alnilam's new leader results in a series of miniature power struggles. For example, the night before the graduation ceremony, Alder tells Shears to "let it ride. . . . We're all the same"; Harbelis remarks, "Don't talk it to death, Shears"; and Thomasovich questions the accuracy of Shears's statements (591). Near the end of the meeting, when Shears "urgently" exclaims, "History will remember it. History damn well will" (597), it becomes evident that instead of "indifference and austerity," Alnilam is founded on willful egotism.

Like the cadets, Frank Cahill is initially driven by destructive egotistical forces. Egotism impels Cahill to show up at the graduation where Alnilam will begin its insurrection. He succumbs to the cadets' desire that he be present not because he has become more sympathetic to their cause, but in defiance of the colonel, who has banned him from the base. Cahill, though at moments intrigued by Alnilam, is essentially skeptical about its mystic pretensions and wary of the cadets' goals. At one point Cahill asks himself, "How can these kids possibly believe this stuff? Even the Boy Scouts were not so ridiculous" (412), and when Shears is explaining Alnilam's secret code he seems "not boyish, but a boy" to Cahill (424). It is not until the scene where the colonel reprimands Cahill for going up in a plane with McCaig and breaking a series of other regulations, and calls Cahill's bluff concerning his relationship with Joel, that Cahill decides not to "give anything away. . . . Don't tell him a damn thing about Shears and the others; not a thing about the boys. Let's let them go ahead" (527). After the blind man claims he is determined to attend the ceremony because "this is gonna be the one thing I ever did for my boy," McLendon tells Cahill "You ain't doin' it for your boy, Frank. That's bullshit. You ain't doin' it for him and you ain't doin' it for the other boys either. You're doin' it for yourself, just like always. You're doin' it because the colonel threw you out" (540). Near the work's conclusion, after he has realized the destructiveness of such egotism, Cahill admits that he did not make the trip to Peckover out of concern for Joel, but for his own self-aggrandizement:

> "I came because . . . because I wanted to know what the hell was goin' on," Cahill said lamely, and then picked up, as he felt himself coming nearer the truth. "I came because I thought maybe it would be hard . . . it would be hard for a man in my shape to do, without nobody helpin' him, without nobody but him and a dog. I felt like I could do it, and wanted to do it, and I felt that it was somethin' that couldn't no other, no other ordinary man. No ordinary blind man anyway." (654)

Dickey's emphasis on the destructiveness of egotism reaches its climax when Cahill's and the cadets' need to see themselves as the "center" causes the graduation day disaster, resulting in an innocent man's death. In an action symbolic of his egotistical need for power, instead of measuring out the insulin to keep his blood "balanced," Cahill, because he "aims to feel stronger," overdoses himself, wanders into the airstrip, and sends the planes crashing into each other, throwing a greater element of chaos into the revolt the cadets had already planned. Moreover, Spain's account of the events suggests the real motivation behind the cadets' rebellious act:

> "I was battling away," Spain said. "Planes were coming at me from the sides, and I could get out of the way but I couldn't catch one to ram him; I couldn't get one in my sights you might could say. I was after getting somebody, anybody I could. They could all take their chances, like I was doing. I got clear, once; I got all the way off the parking area and on to the dirt, and was clear of the whole place, the whole area where the planes were tearing into each other and all hell had done been turned loose. But I went back in. I hadn't had enough; I couldn't get enough." (638–39)

Spain's comments indicate that his primary goal, like the other Alnilam cadets', is not staging a rebellion that would facilitate their stated purpose of bringing about the "end of everything that's ever been wrong," but to glorify his own assertion of power. By showing power and ego, rather than ideas and morals, as the inescapable driving forces behind the cadets' nonconformity, Dickey erodes and undermines the legitimacy of the protest. Spain does not pursue a particular person or thing, but is bent on destructive anarchy ("anybody I could get"), resulting in a display of egotistical "evil" and helping to create a place where "all hell had been turned loose." In stark contrast to a world where eliminating "everything that has ever been wrong" is possible, Dickey presents a world where everyone is party to its "secret little evils" (648).

Dickey creates a link between Cahill's desires for consequentiality and egotistical destructiveness through his attempts at "imaging." Because of his faith in images' power for revelation, Cahill thinks he can make himself "the center of the outside world . . . and because of this he believed that he had an authentic image—a vision full of power, certainty, control, and delight" (92). Nevertheless, as Adel Bledsoe tells him while reading his palm and the lines around his eyes, "There's something that you can't control. . . . You think you can, but you can't. . . . It's got to do with what you know, with your education, like. It's gonna be hard for you to learn. . . . There's gonna be something you can't get at, and you might want to. That part might not be too good, for you" (280–81, 283).

Like the golden streaks of light that continuously shuttle before the blind man, and "seem like they're comin' from way deep down," but do "not form anything solid," despite the effort of the "ceaseless jerking of his eyeballs" trying "to follow what cannot be followed," Cahill's imagination pursues his images until he feels on the brink of a revelation that never comes—at least not in a manner immediately apparent to Cahill (1). For instance, while listening to Colonel Hoccleave over the public-address system, Cahill senses he is about to be "delivered of something ultimate," but as he concentrates on an image of a girl with a ball in her hand, "with the awaited word she vanished" (61).

After several similar frustrations, Cahill's attempts "to image" culminate in the episode where he and McCaig fly the airplane. The sensations during the flight intoxicate Cahill with the potential of his own power. He feels that "there might in some way be a presence, a sign waiting to be released," and, as McCaig gives him control of the aircraft, he glories in the fact that "the whole thing is mine; it's all mine" (491, 492). As this sense of power grows he believes he is once more on the verge of revelation: "In there, where nothing could live, a figure materialized in and out in pieces: first a short horned head, then an arm and a hand with still fingers, two unrelated leaping legs, a torso settling itself between them and quivering out of relation, then all of these together, then none, then almost all again, dancing ironically, not hurting, beyond Cahill's pain, pitiless, homeless, imperious" (495).

When this vision disappears and a series of other images also fail to reveal anything, he screams, "God-damn you. . . . This is the same god-damn thing. I almost . . . I ain't going with this no more" (497), and he sends the plane downward in a suicidal plunge. Though Cahill feels he "never did have" the vision, and tries to explain the self-destructive act as an attempt to capture it, McCaig provides him with a more accurate assessment. McCaig, who wants to know "what the hell had a-holt of you. . . . What the hell did you think you was doin'?" tells Cahill, "It's the meanness of your god-damned will power. . . . It's your god-damned will power" (513). Indeed, the vision of "a horned fire demon," "a creature who had lived some-where within" Cahill, represents the destructive evil of his—and Joel's—egotism (506).

Dickey's concluding scenes suggest how to "draw the line be-tween what you can use and what's liable to hurt you," by dra-matizing the differences between Cahill and the cadets. The gradu-ation day disaster enables Cahill to realize the destructiveness of his own egotism, so he confines "imaging" to forms of self-exploration. But unlike Cahill, who likes "to build in . . . where don't nobody but you know what the hell is going on," Joel's followers continue to use poetry and their egotistical impulses in subordination to their political causes (572). After he realizes his own potential for "evil," Cahill serves to mediate between the "idealistic" and the "practi-cal." When Hoccleave enters the infirmary to question Cahill, the blind man is no longer confrontational but offers his hand as a gesture of amends. After Hoccleve tells him that Faulstick was killed as a result of the graduation day "accident," Cahill, for the first time in the novel, apologizes, telling the Colonel, "This'n didn't

have to happen. . . . Not a damn bit, it didn't. It was my boy's doin'.
In some kind of way it was. I'm sorry" (632). Similarly, he tells Dr.
Iannone that he will now "do what [the doctors] tell me," in order to
keep his blood "balanced" (648).

Despite these concessions, Cahill does not completely accept the
conventional positions that Iannone and Hoccleave prescribe, refus-
ing to provide either of them with any information concerning
Alnilam, though in private he threatens Shears that if any more
violence ensues he will "stop" Alnilam and "come after" him "no
matter what" (667). Unlike the Alnilam cadets, Cahill is able to face
the evil of his willful egotism and become part of the human com-
munity. In contrast, the cadets continue to believe that like Alnilam,
the middle star in the constellation Orion, they are the center, they
can have "all we want" (651, 665); but as Whitehall explains, the star
Alnilam is "not much used in navigation" because "there are lots
better ones" (655). Accordingly, Cahill finally declares, "I ain't the
center of anything," announces that he will now "go with people,"
and makes gestures toward initiating human relationships by invit-
ing McLendon and Hannah to Atlanta, and by confirming the im-
portance of his relationship with Ruiz (651, 676).

Like *Deliverance* and his poems, *Alnilam* represents a chapter in
Dickey's exploration of "the relationship between sources of power
and the imagination."[16] As Peggy Goodman Endel has observed,
Dickey's "work has always possessed a powerful, anti-romantic
concern with a moral evil that exists in tension with the Romantic
sublime."[17] Dickey has claimed that he wants "to burst through to
some magnificent region of the human personality and the creative
mind which will no longer have any debits but which will be all
positive," but his sense of the inherent evil in humankind is so
strong that he often views idealistic impulses with suspicion (*NH*,
263). In *Alnilam*, even Dickey's paragon of human potential—the
energized man—is portrayed as flawed and destructive. Instead of
reforming society, Dickey's characters can only hope to confirm that
they "mean"—"that there is a place the universe can't deny you"—
and use their imaginations to come to grips with where they stand

16. James Dickey, letter to author, April 18, 1989.
17. "Dickey, Dante, and the Demonic," 611–12.

between "the Devil and the Lord put together," between "death and damnation" (662, 654).

In its emphasis on the personal nature of Cahill's romantic impulses and on the dangers of seeking to transcend mundane reality, *Alnilam* also typifies Dickey's work. By creating a distinction between Frank Cahill's use of his imagination for personal self-realization and the cadets' use of their imaginative faculties for social purposes— for bringing about the "end of everything that's ever been wrong"— Dickey is not only commenting on the incompatibility of the artistic enterprise with political action, but also expressing his wariness toward idealism, an attitude that can be directly linked to his belief in humans' inherent potential for evil. The military and social bureaucracies are depicted as stultifying in their authoritarian emphasis on conformity, and dangerous in the ends they wish to achieve through demanding that conformity. Whitehall, whom Cahill calls a "preacher," ominously reminds us, "Every one of these boys is being taught to kill" so that they can become "the kings of death" (645). On the other hand, revolts against the system are portrayed as naive, fanatical, destructive, power-obsessed, and egotistically grandiose. The mystical rebels of Alnilam are portrayed in the end as egotists involved in a game of naive power playing, whose need to feel consequential makes them vulnerable to the manipulations of a charismatic leader. Notably, the type of people Cahill decides "to go with" in the end—McLendon, Hannah, Ruiz— are those who are not in any way involved in the political spectrum, but those who aid Cahill for reasons of friendship, rather than because of his usefulness to a cause. Even Cahill's "buddy," McCaig, who eventually joins the war effort, is not depicted as a soldier, but as a crop-dusting pilot who wants to fly overseas in order to escape the bureaucratic and political intrigues of the military establishment. Indeed, looking at *Alnilam* and at Dickey's use of personae to examine the relationship between romanticism and hedonism reflects his insistence that he has "no particular interest in talking about politics," and that "enthusiasm and a personal stake in the realm of the imagination" are "the only things that matter," unpopular claims among today's politically hypersensitive critics.

The Dickey oeuvre demonstrates how the techniques and trends that characterize an era can influence interpretations of a writer's work, particularly when the writer is operating outside dominant modes. Dickey often uses a line from "Buckdancer's Choice" to characterize his writings: "A thousand variations of one song," declaring that his method is "not to go wide but narrow and deep," a claim that is verified by considering his work in its entirety. Whether Dickey is using personal experiences, newspaper accounts, purely imaginative occurrences, or other sources as a basis for his poems, his search for multiple perspectives and situations that explore the compulsion for consequentiality remains a distinctive constant. Critics' propensity to view Dickey's poetry and public image as inextricable from contemporary reactions against the use of persona has prevented them from recognizing his persistent examination of the romantic impulse for meaning, as well as his analysis of the dangers and rewards of this quest. Indeed, the web of historical and literary trends that have motivated interpretations and misinterpretations of Dickey's public image, his relationship to mass culture, his southernness, his poetic origins, his politics, his techniques, and his themes reveals how the vicissitudes of the politics of canon have resulted in his critical reputation's flow and ebb.

With two new books of poetry—*Real God, Roll* and *Peace Raids*—and a new novel, *To the White Sea,* ready for release,–James Dickey will surely continue to be a vital voice in contemporary letters. What seems more problematical is how seriously, and how widely, his work is likely to be read as time passes. During the last twenty years his reputation among ideologically conscious critics has certainly not fared well. And though his "assumed personality" has brought him a great deal of publicity, it has often made critics focus on his personal antics, rather than his writing, or caused critics to mistakenly view his work through his public image. The seventies were especially damaging in this regard. *Deliverance*—novel and movie—generated much notoriety. *Self-Interviews* and *Sorties* focused on his personal life, as did numerous articles and television shows, especially after Jimmy Carter summoned him to read at the inaugural celebration. That Dickey published most of his poorest poetry—including the confessional verse—during this time, further contributed to critics' skepticism.

Even through this period, however, poets continued to see things in Dickey's work that many critics did not, as becomes evident by looking at a small sample of the praise he received. In May 1970 Ann Stanford wrote him to express her great admiration for his work and to send him a poem, "To a Poet (for James Dickey)," that she had written in his honor. In a letter dated December 21, 1970, James Wright declared that he believed Dickey was "the greatest poet of my time." On April 17, 1971, Karl Shapiro wrote that Dickey was "one of the best poets in America." In a letter to Dickey dated May 18, 1974, Robert Lowell, who had offered to edit Dickey's uncollected papers, asserted that Dickey and Peter Taylor were the last important southern writers. On June 6, 1978, Elder Olson, who was teaching at the University of Chicago, wrote to Robert Hill, coeditor of the *South Carolina Review,* and claimed that Dickey was "one of the very finest, if not the finest, of living poets." William Stafford, on May 19, 1980, sent Dickey a poem inspired by the way in which Dickey's poems have "strobe-lighted along through my days. . . . Now and then I have tried to express the vividness that you have struck into being."

What qualities in Dickey's work moved Stanford, Wright, Shapiro, Lowell, Olson, Stafford, and others—in letters spanning from 1970 to 1980, a period during which even critics who admired Dickey's work felt he had slipped—to write him expressing their admiration? Dickey has founded no "school" or movement. Unlike Ezra Pound, Robert Bly, or Charles Olson, he has not sought to direct other writers' craft by espousing poetic theories or editing their work. Dickey does just the opposite: he insists on his own independence and berates imitators. Oddly enough, the key to comprehending other writers' continued admiration for Dickey may well reside in this independence, as suggested by James Wright's assertion to Dickey: "The enemy of poetry is the clever champion of a 'literary school.' That's why I phoned you. You aren't a school. You're James Dickey."

Nevertheless, as with Hemingway, separating the public image from the work will be difficult, no matter how other poets view Dickey's work. Dickey now regrets "encouraging and allowing" the mass cultivation of his public image, calling it his greatest "mistake," and wants the emphasis placed on his writing (*VC*, 237). So on to the heart of the matter: while Dickey may well be the South's favored man and be an important figure to his peers, how does a writer's work live if the institution in charge of tradition has decided against it? If his new work further elaborates a vision of life out-of-step with the values motivating literary criticism, Dickey's writing will continue in its current paradoxical impasse: it will be widely accepted and read, especially in the South, but will be given only marginal attention by the academy. At the same time, studies such as Bloom's *James Dickey* and Kirschten's *James Dickey and the Gentle Ecstasy of Earth* suggest that serious attention to Dickey's poetry and fiction is on the rise, and one may speculate that Dickey will emerge once more as a major writer if literary assessments again come to focus on the power inherent in a writer's craft, quite apart from critics' perceptions of a writer's political ideology.

Another possibility seems more likely, however. Ironically, the longevity of Dickey's reputation may reside in the very characteristics that critics find objectionable, an observation that can be brought into focus by considering Lionel Trilling's "The Meaning of a Literary Idea." Trilling distinguishes an "idea" from an "ideology" by claiming, "Ideology is not a product of thought; it is the habit or the ritual of showing respect for certain formulas to which, for various reasons having to do with emotional safety, we have strong ties." He goes on to tout Faulkner and Hemingway as more important writers than Dos Passos, with whom Trilling shared many political sympathies, because they "insisted on their indifference to the conscious intellectual tradition of our time and have acquired the reputation of achieving their effects by means that have the least possible connection with any sort of intellectuality or even with intelligence." Trilling points to the "activity" with which they tackle "the recalcitrant stuff of life," a quality that provides "the distinct impression that the two novelists are not under any illusion that they have conquered the material upon which they direct their activity."[18]

Similarly, the sensationalistic and contradictory currents that run through Dickey's writing are richly complex expressions of the paradoxes present in American culture and the human condition. Dickey expresses our culture's violence, destructiveness, and illu-

18. *The Liberal Imagination: Essays on Literature and Society,* 286, 296, 297.

sions of grandeur, as well as its ebullience and its insatiable deter-
mination to keep striving for images of reality that connect with our
ideals. Yet his willingness to explore fundamental impulses from a
variety of perspectives has generated a body of work that today's
academy cannot accommodate. Rather than recognizing that a writer's
ability to address the very things that make us uncomfortable tests
ideological boundaries, critics have lapsed into judging literature
according to the New Left's ideological premises. But if capturing a
culture's emotional dimensions becomes a measure of status, then,
among American poets, perhaps only Whitman matches Dickey's
imaginative power and ambition, for Dickey's work reflects his
relentless drive to confront more and more experience.

While reading about Frank Cahill and the imminence of revela-
tion, I wondered if Dickey has not been somehow disappointed that
in all these years he has not experienced revelation, some kind of
Old Testament vision, that he expected his poetry or his life to yield,
and that would allow him to deliver the "immortal message to
mankind" he spoke of in *Sorties*. His relatively recent poem "Cir-
cuit" speaks to this point:

> Beaches; it is true: they go on   oń
> And on, but as they ram and pack, foreseeing
>
> Around a curve, always   slow-going headlong
>
>   For the circle
>   swerving from water
> But not really, their minds on a perfect connection, no matter
>   How long it takes. You can't be
>   On them without making the choice
>   To meet yourself no matter
>
>   How long. Don't be afraid;
>   It will come   will hit you
>
>   Straight out of the wind, on wings or not,
>   Where you have blanked yourself
>
>   Still with your feet.

As the narrator meditates on the "perfect connection," the time-
less (they go on   oń / And on), intricate, and inviolable order of
natural processes, he discovers it impossible not to consider the

self's relationship to those processes and what message they hold for him. Motionless, he empties his consciousness to await revelation:

> there are only
> In one shallow spray-pool   thís one
>
> Strong horses circling. Stretch and tell me, Lord;
> Let the place talk.
>
> This may just be it.

Looking into the spray-pool's current, the narrator makes an impassioned plea for meaning, consequence, a positive assessment of the savage ideal, but the poem concludes with this expression of desire. When I asked Dickey why the poem ended as it did, his countenance changed from a joyful intensity to dead seriousness. "Because those things can't happen," he replied, vividly expressing a universal ache, as well as the thing to which his work testifies: the importance of an individual's search for meaning in the here and now, a poetic and spiritual act that cannot remain very long out of fashion.

Bibliography

Works by James Dickey

Alnilam. Garden City, N.Y.: Doubleday, 1987.

"The Anniversary." *Poetry* 82 (June 1953): 138–39.

Babel to Byzantium: Poets and Poetry Now. New York: Farrar, Straus and Giroux, 1968.

"Barnstorming for Poetry." In *Babel to Byzantium: Poets and Poetry Now*. New York: Farrar, Straus and Giroux, 1968.

Buckdancer's Choice. Middletown, Conn.: Wesleyan University Press, 1965.

The Central Motion. Middletown, Conn.: Wesleyan University Press, 1983.

"The Child in Armour." *Poetry* 82 (June 1953): 137.

"Comments to Accompany *Poems, 1957–1967*." *Barat Review* 3 (January 1968): 9–15.

Deliverance. Boston: Houghton Mifflin, 1970.

Drowning with Others. Middletown, Conn.: Wesleyan University Press, 1962.

The Eagle's Mile. Middletown, Conn.: Wesleyan University Press, 1990.

The Early Motion. Middletown, Conn.: Wesleyan University Press, 1981.

"The Energized Man." In *The Imagination as Glory: Essays on the Poetry of James Dickey*, edited by Bruce Weigl and T. R. Hummer, 163–64. Urbana and Chicago: University of Illinois Press, 1984.

The Eye-Beaters, Blood, Victory, Madness, Buckhead, and Mercy. Garden City, N.Y.: Doubleday, 1970.

Falling, May Day Sermon, and Other Poems. Middletown, Conn.: Wesleyan University Press, 1981.

"The Father's Body." *Poetry* 89 (December 1956): 145–49.

"From Babel to Byzantium." *Sewanee Review* 62 (July–September 1957): 508–30.

"The Ground of Killing." *Sewanee Review* 62 (October 1954): 623–24.

Helmets. Middletown, Conn.: Wesleyan University Press, 1964.

"The Imagination as Glory." In *The Imagination as Glory: Essays on the Poetry of James Dickey,* edited by Bruce Weigl and T. R. Hummer, 166–73. Urbana and Chicago: University of Illinois Press, 1984.

Into the Stone and Other Poems. In *Poets of Today 7,* edited by John Hall. Wheelock, N.Y.: Scribners, 1960.

Metaphor as Pure Adventure: A Lecture Delivered at the Library of Congress, December 4, 1967. Washington, D.C.: Library of Congress, 1968. Reprinted in *Sorties.* Garden City, N.Y.: Doubleday, 1971.

Night Hurdling. Columbia and Bloomfield Hills, S.C.: Bruccoli Clark, 1983.

"Of Holy War." *Poetry* 79 (1951): 24.

Poems, 1957–1967. Middletown, Conn.: Wesleyan University Press, 1967.

Puella. Garden City, N.Y.: Doubleday, 1982.

Self-Interviews. Edited by Barbara and James Reiss. Garden City, N.Y.: Doubleday, 1970.

"The Shark in the Window." *Sewanee Review* 59 (April–June 1951): 290–91.

Sorties. Garden City, N.Y.: Doubleday, 1971.

Spinning the Crystal Ball. Washington, D.C.: Library of Congress, 1967.

"The String." *Poetry* 94 (July 1959): 222–23.

The Suspect in Poetry. Madison, Minn.: Sixties Press, 1964.

"The Suspect in Poetry or Everyman as Detective." *Sewanee Review* 68 (October–December 1960): 660–74.

"To Be Edward Thomas." *Beloit Poetry Journal Chapbook* 5 (Summer 1957): 10–15.

Two Poems of the Air. Portland: Centicore Press, 1964.

The Voiced Connections of James Dickey. Columbia: University of South Carolina Press, 1989.

Interviews with James Dickey

"An Interview with James Dickey." Interview with author. *Contemporary Literature* 31 (Summer 1990): 116–32.

Interviews with author. August 8–15, 1989. Tape recording.

"James Dickey." Interview in *Writers at Work: The Paris Review Interviews*, 5th series, edited by George Plimpton, 199–229. New York: Viking Press, 1981.

"James Dickey: Interview." *Unmuzzled Ox* 2 (1975): 77–85.

Other Works Cited

Achebe, Chinua. "An Image of Africa: Racism in Conrad's *Heart of Darkness.*" *The Massachusetts Review* 18 (1977): 782–94.

Altieri, Charles. *Enlarging the Temple: New Directions in American Poetry.* Lewisburg, Pa.: Bucknell University Press, 1979.

———. "From Symbolist Thought to Immanence: The Logic of Postmodern Poetics." *Boundary* 2 1 (1973): 605–41.

Arnett, David Leslie. "James Dickey: Poetry and Fiction." Ph.D. diss., Tulane University, 1973.

Axelrod, Steven Gould. *Robert Lowell: Life and Art.* Princeton: Princeton University Press, 1978.

Bartlett, Lee, ed. *Talking Poetry: Conversations in the Workshop with Contemporary Poets.* Albuquerque: University of New Mexico Press, 1987.

Bartlett, Lee, and Hugh Witemeyer. "Ezra Pound and James Dickey: A Correspondence and a Kinship." *Paideuma* 82 (June 1983): 290–312.

Baughman, Ronald. *Understanding James Dickey.* Columbia: University of South Carolina Press, 1985.

Bennett, Ross. "'The Firebombing': A Reappraisal." *American Literature* 52, no. 3 (November 1980): 430–48.

Bernstein, Richard. "The Rising Hegemony of the Politically Correct." *New York Times,* October 28, 1980, 4, 1:1.

Bloom, Harold, ed. *James Dickey: Modern Critical Views.* New York: Chelsea, 1987.

Bly, Robert [Crunk, pseud.]. "Buckdancer's Choice." *Sixties* 9 (Spring 1967): 70–79.

———. "Interview." *The Lamp in the Spine* 3 (Winter 1972): 50–65.

———. "Prose vs. Poetry." *Choice* 2 (1962): 65–80.

———. "The Work of James Dickey." *Sixties* 7 (Winter 1964): 41–57.

Bowers, Neal. *James Dickey: The Poet as Pitchman.* Columbia: University of Missouri Press, 1985.

Breslin, James E. B. *From Modern to Contemporary: American Poetry, 1945–1965.* Chicago: University of Chicago Press, 1984.

Breslin, Paul. *The Psycho-Political Muse: American Poetry since the Fifties.* Chicago: University of Chicago Press, 1987.

Broyard, Anatole. "Dickey's Likes and Dislikes." *New York Times,* December 17, 1971, 37.

Calhoun, Richard. "On Robert Bly's Protest Poetry." *Tennessee Poetry Journal* 2 (Winter 1969): 21–22.

———. "Whatever Happened to the Poet Critic?" *Southern Literary Journal* 1 (Fall 1968): 75–88.

———, ed. *James Dickey: The Expansive Imagination.* Delano, Fla.: Everett Edwards, 1973.

Calhoun, Richard, and Robert W. Hill. *James Dickey.* Boston: Twayne Publishers, 1983.

Carroll, Paul. "James Dickey as Critic." *Chicago Review,* November 20, 1968, 82–87.

———. *The Poem in Its Skin.* Chicago: Follett Press, 1968.

Cash, W. J. *The Mind of the South.* New York: Alfred Knopf, 1941.

Cleaver, Eldridge. *Soul on Ice.* New York: Dell, 1968.

Covel, Robert C. "A Starry Place: The Energized Man in *Alnilam.*" *James Dickey Newsletter* 5 (Spring 1989): 5–17.

Davison, Peter. "The Difficulties of Being Major" *Atlantic* 220 (October 1967): 116–21.

DeVoto, Bernard. "Witchcraft in Mississippi." *Saturday Review of Literature,* October 31, 1936, 3–4, 14.

Dodsworth, Martin. "Towards the Baseball Poem." *Listener* 79 (June 27, 1968): 842.

Ellmann, Mary. *Thinking about Women.* New York: Harcourt Brace, 1968.

Emerson, Ralph Waldo. *Selections from Ralph Waldo Emerson.* Edited by Stephen E. Whicher. Boston: Houghton Mifflin, 1957.

Endel, Peggy Goodman. "Dickey, Dante, and the Demonic: Reassessing *Deliverance.*" *American Literature* 60.4 (December 1988): 611–24.

Fass, Ekbert. *Towards a New American Poetics: Essays and Interviews.* Santa Barbara, Calif.: Black Sparrow Press, 1978.

Friebert, Stuart, and David Young, eds. *A Field Guide to Contemporary Poetry and Poetics.* New York: Longman, 1980.

Geismar, Maxwell. *Writers in Crisis: The American Novel, 1925–1940.* New York: Houghton Mifflin Company, 1942.

Gilbert, Sandra M., and Susan Gubar. "Feminism and Literature: An Exchange." *New York Review of Books,* August 16, 1990, 58–59.

Ginsberg, Allen. *Allen Verbatim: Lectures on Poetry, Politics, Consciousness.* Edited by Gordon Ball. New York: McGraw-Hill, 1974.

———. "Notebooks, 1953–1956." In *Journals: Early Fifties, Early Sixties*, edited by Gordon Ball. New York: Grove Press, 1977.

Glauber, Robert, and Chad Walsh. "Why Another 'Little Magazine'?" *Beloit Poetry Journal Chapbook* 1 (Fall 1950): 1–2.

Goldman, Michael. "Inventing the American Heart." *Nation* 204 (April 24, 1967): 529–30.

Hartwick, Harry. *The Foreground of American Fiction*. New York: American Book, 1934.

Hicks, Granville. *The Great Tradition: An Interpretation of American Literature since the Civil War*. New York: Macmillan, 1935.

Hill, Robert W. "Editorial." *South Carolina Review* 10 (April 1978): 2–3.

Holden, Jonathan. *Style and Authenticity in Postmodern Poetry*. Columbia: University of Missouri Press, 1986.

Howard, Richard. *Alone with America: Essays on the Art of Poetry in the United States Since 1950*. New York: Atheneum, 1969. Expanded edition 1980.

Jameson, Fredric. "The Great American Hunter or Ideological Content in the Novel." *College English* 34 (November 1972): 180–97.

Keller, Lynn. *Re-Making It New: Contemporary American Poetry and the Modernist Tradition*. Cambridge: Harvard University Press, 1987.

Kennedy, X. J. "Joys, Griefs, and 'All Things Innocent, Hapless, Forsaken.'" *New York Times Book Review*, August 23, 1964, 5.

Kerley, Gary. "Unifying the Energy and Balancing the Vision." *James Dickey Newsletter* 5 (Spring 1989): 17–26.

Kinnell, Galway. "Poetry, Personality, and Death." In *A Field Guide to Contemporary Poetry and Poetics*, edited by Stuart Friebert and David Young, 203–23. New York: Longman, 1980.

Kirschten, Robert. *James Dickey and the Gentle Ecstasy of Earth: A Reading of the Poems*. Baton Rouge: Louisiana State University Press, 1988.

Kramer, Jane. *Allen Ginsberg in America*. New York: Random House, 1969.

Krystal, Arthur. "Reloading the Canon." *Book World*, February 16, 1992, 10, 14.

Libby, Anthony. "Fire and Light: Four Poets to the End and Beyond." *Iowa Review* 4 (Spring 1973): 111–26.

Lowell, Robert. "The Art of Poetry." In *Robert Lowell: A Collection of Critical Essays*, edited by Thomas Parkinson, 19–36. Englewood Cliffs, N.J.: Prentice-Hall, 1968.

———. "For John Berryman." *New York Review of Books*, April 6, 1972, 3–4.

———. "Thomas, Bishop, and Williams." *Sewanee Review* 55 (July–September 1947): 492–98.

———. "Visiting the Tates." *Sewanee Review* 67 (Autumn 1959): 557–59.

Malkoff, Karl. *Crowell's Handbook of Contemporary American Poetry*. New York: Thomas Crowell, 1973.

———. *Escape from the Self*. New York: Columbia University Press, 1977.

Mazzaro, Jerome, *Postmodern American Poetry*. Urbana and Chicago: University of Illinois Press, 1980.

Meredith, William. "A Good Time for All," *New York Times Book Review*, April 23, 1967, 4, 46.

Mesic, Michael. "A Note on James Dickey." In *American Poetry Since 1960*, edited by Robert B. Shaw, 145–53. Chester Springs, Pa.: Dufour, 1974.

Mills, Ralph J. "Brilliant Essays on Contemporary Poetry." *Chicago Sun-Times Book Week*, May 5, 1968, 4. Reprinted in *Cry of the Human: Essays on Contemporary American Poetry*. Urbana and Chicago: University of Illinois Press, 1974.

———. *Creation's Very Self: On the Personal Element in Recent American Poetry*. Fort Worth: Texas Christian University Press, 1969.

———. "The Poetry of James Dickey." *Triquarterly* 11 (Winter 1968): 231–42.

Molesworth, Charles. *The Fierce Embrace: A Study of Contemporary American Poetry*. Columbia: University of Missouri Press, 1979.

Morris, Robert. "Dueling Dickeys." *Creative Loafing* 20 (December 14, 1991): 17–27, 29.

Nelson, Cary. *Our First Last Poets: Vision and History in Contemporary American Poetry*. Urbana and Chicago: University of Illinois Press, 1981.

Oates, Joyce Carol. "Out of the Stone, into the Flesh: The Imagination of James Dickey." In *New Heaven, New Earth: The Visionary Experience in Literature*, 205–63. New York: Vanguard Press, 1974.

Olson, Charles. *Charles Olson and Ezra Pound: An Encounter at St. Elizabeths*, edited by Catherine Seelye. New York: Grossman Publishers, 1975.

O'Neil, Paul. "The Unlikeliest Poet." *Life* 61 (July 22, 1966): 68–79.

Paglia, Camille. "Ninnies, Pedants, Tyrants, and Other Academics." *New York Times Book Review*, May 5, 1991, 1, 29, 33.

Paul, Sherman. *The Lost America of Love: Rereading Robert Creeley, Edward Dorn, and Robert Duncan*. Baton Rouge: Louisiana State University Press, 1981.

———. *Olson's Push: Origin, Black Mountain, and Recent American Poetry*. Baton Rouge: Louisiana State University Press, 1978.

"Poet James Dickey on Carter and the Born-Again South." *US News and World Report*, April 18, 1977, 67.

Poulin, A., Jr. "Contemporary American Poetry: The Radical Tradition." In *Contemporary American Poetry*, 685–703. Boston: Houghton Mifflin, 1985.

Pound, Ezra. "A Retrospect." In *The Literary Essays of Ezra Pound*, edited by T. S. Eliot, 3–14. London: Faber and Faber, 1954.

Rexroth, Kenneth. *The Alternate Society: Essays from the Other World.* New York: Herder and Herder, 1970.

Rich, Adrienne. "Poetry, Personality, and Wholeness." In *A Field Guide to Contemporary Poetry and Poetics*, edited by Stuart Friebert and David Young, 224–31. New York: Longman, 1980.

Robbins, Fred Walker. "The Poetry of James Dickey, 1951–1967." Ph.D. diss., University of Texas, 1970.

Rosenthal, M. L. *The Modern Poetic Sequence: The Genius of Modern Poetry.* New York: Oxford University Press, 1983.

———. *The New Poets.* New York: Oxford University Press, 1967.

Rubin, Louis, Jr. *The Wary Fugitives: Four Poets and the South.* Baton Rouge: Louisiana State University Press, 1978.

Silverstein, Norman. "James Dickey's Muscular Eschatology." *Salmagund*, no. 22–23 (Spring–Summer 1973): 258–68. Reprinted in *Contemporary Poetry in America*, edited by Robert Boyers, 303–13. New York: Schocken Books, 1974.

Stitt, Peter. *The Beauty of the World's Hieroglyphics: Four American Poets.* Athens: University of Georgia Press, 1978.

Sugg, Richard. *Robert Bly.* Boston: Twayne Publishers, 1986.

Sullivan, Walter. *A Requiem for the Renaissance: The State of Fiction in the Modern South.* Athens: University of Georgia Press, 1976.

Thwaite, Anthony. "Out of Bondage." *New Statesman* 80 (September 11, 1970): 310–11.

Trilling, Lionel. *The Liberal Imagination: Essays on Literature and Society.* New York: Viking Press, 1950.

Van Ness, Arthur Gordon. "Ritual Magic." Ph.D. diss., University of South Carolina, 1987.

Von Hallberg, Robert. *American Poetry and Culture, 1945–1980.* Cambridge: Harvard University Press, 1985.

Waggoner, Hyatt H. *American Poetry from the Puritans to the Present.* Baton Rouge: Louisiana State University Press, 1984.

Weatherby, H. L. "The Way of Exchange in James Dickey's Poetry." *Hudson Review* 74 (July–September 1966): 669–80.

Weigl, Bruce, and T. R. Hummer, eds. *The Imagination as Glory: Essays on the Poetry of James Dickey.* Urbana and Chicago: University of Illinois Press, 1984.

Wellek, Rene. *Concepts of Criticism: Essays.* Edited by Stephen G. Nichols, Jr. New Haven, Conn.: Yale University Press, 1963.

Williams. Harry. *The Edge Is What I Have: Theodore Roethke and After.* Lewisburg, Penn.: Bucknell University Press, 1978.

Winters, Yvor. *In Defense of Reason: Primitivism and Decadence.* Denver: University of Denver Press, 1947.

The Writer and His Tradition. Knoxville: University of Tennessee Press, 1969.

Young, David. "The Bite of the Muskrat: Judging Contemporary Poetry." In *A Field Guide to Contemporary Poetry and Poetics,* edited by Stuart Friebert and David Young, 123–34. New York: Longman, 1980.

Young-Bruehl, Elizabeth. "Pride and Prejudice." *Lingua Franca* 1 (February 1991): 15–18.

Index